TRAIN YOUR OWN GPT

HOW TO TRAIN CHATGPT TO THINK LIKE YOU

FROM MrEXCEL/BILL JELEN

MrGPT PRESS

PO Box 541731, Merritt Island FL 32954

Train Your Own GPT

First Publication: August 1, 2025

Authors: Bill Jelen

Indexer: Nellie Jay

Compositor: Jill Cabot

Copy Editor: Conni A. Secrets

Cover Design: Kim Sekas

Published by: Holy Macro! Books, PO Box 541731, Merritt Island FL 32954

Distributed by Independent Publishers Group, Chicago, IL

ISBN 978-1-61547-090-7 (print) 978-1-61547-177-5 (digital)

Version 20250812a

Table of Contents

Dedication

To the Kraut King, my departed Uncle Mike - He was 50 years ahead of his time

Thanks to

Suat Ozgur. Kim Sekas. Stacie Fuss, Alina Bankal, Susan Hutt, Janice Back, Nabil Mourad, ChatGPT, and Mary Ellen Jelen

About the Author

Bill Jelen is the host of MrExcel.com and the author of 71 books about Microsoft Excel including *Excel Gurus Gone Wild and Excel Pivot Table Data Crunching* for Microsoft Press. He has made over 80 guest appearances on TV's *The Lab with Leo / Call for Help with Leo Laporte* and was voted guest of the year on the *Computer America* radio show. He wrote the Excel column for *Strategic Finance* magazine. He has produced over 2,600 episodes of his daily video podcast Learn Excel from MrExcel. Social Media:

- YouTube: https://www.youtube.com/@MrXL
- X: https://x.com/MrExcel
- LinkedIn: https://www.linkedin.com/in/billjelen/
- Facebook: https://www.facebook.com/MrExcelSpeaker
- Instagram: https://www.instagram.com/mrexcelbill/
- Threads: https://www.threads.net/@mrexcelbill
- Pinterest: https://www.pinterest.com/mrexcel/
- Website Excel: https://www.mrexcel.com/
- Website GPT: https://www.mrgpt.pro/

Sample File Downloads

The files used in this book are available for download from

mrx.cl/gptbookfiles.

The Chapter One Goal Statement

Let's build a GPT — you and me,
By Chapter One, you'll set it free.
No code, no stress, just step-by-step,
You'll train your own AI adept.

But first, a stop at Chapter Zero,
It's short — no cape, no masked hero.
A few key points to warm the flow,
So don't you dare just skip and go.

Your first big win? It's close at hand.
Soon, your GPT will understand.
By Chapter One, you'll take the lead—
Build your own GPT with lightning speed!

Foreword

The original plan for this book had you building your first GPT in Chapter 6. But here's the truth: if you're using ChatGPT Plus, you can have something useful running before the end of Chapter 1.

So, I restructured everything.

We start with a quick Chapter Zero to lay some groundwork. After that, Chapters 1 through 9 each walk you through a specific GPT I've built — real examples, real outcomes, no fluff. My goal is simple: show you how to take your GPT idea and bring it to life in about 20 minutes.

The most important ingredient? Confidence.

This will work.

Maybe not perfectly the first time. But by version 2? You'll be smiling. And your GPT will be doing 90% of what you imagined.

I spent a lot of time with ChatGPT while writing this book. We're basically bros now. Along the way, we had a few exchanges that made me laugh out loud. You'll find some of those scattered throughout the book — just for fun — formatted like this:

> Bill: Can I give my GPT a cape and a theme song?
>
> ChatGPT: Capes are optional, but a theme song is encouraged. Just make sure it's in Markdown.

#0 Introduction Why I Wrote This Book

I've been teaching Excel for over 25 years. I've written more than 70 books, created thousands of videos, answered countless questions, and along the way, found a way to make formulas, charts, and pivot tables… actually kind of fun.

And then along came ChatGPT.

At first, I wasn't sure what to make of it. Was it a gimmick? Was it a threat to everything I'd built? Was it going to take my job?

Turns out, it's none of those things.

Well… maybe one of those things. We'll get to that.

What I've learned is this: AI is here, and it's changing how people work. And the sooner we learn to work with it instead of worrying about it, the better off we'll be.

This book isn't about AI theory. It's not about how to build neural networks or train language models from scratch. You don't need a computer science degree. You don't even need to know how to code.

What you need is curiosity. And maybe a little patience.

What You'll Learn

In the chapters ahead, I'm going to show you how to create something called a Custom GPT — a version of ChatGPT that you can train to work the way you want. I will also touch on the similar process to create a Custom Agent in Microsoft Copilot.

You'll learn how to:

- Write better instructions (so it actually listens)
- Give your GPT memory, style, and tone
- Feed it your own data
- Automate tasks you thought only humans could do
- Use it as a research assistant, writing partner, transcript formatter, or whatever else you can dream up

I'll walk through real examples I've built — some for Excel, some for YouTube, and some just for fun.

Why Now?

Here's the honest part: this book is a bit of a pivot.

For nearly three decades, I've been in the business of teaching people how to be more efficient when using Microsoft Excel. Millions of people searched for Excel help on Google, found our site. It worked. It paid the bills. It let me keep teaching.

But these days, people don't click through to my site as often. Google's AI answers show up at the top, and folks get what they need without ever visiting the page.

So yes, there's irony here: I'm writing a book about how to use the very technology that's replacing my old business model.

But that's the point.

This isn't a book about resisting change. It's a book about understanding it—and using it to build something new.

Who This Book Is For

This book is for:

- Anyone curious about AI but unsure where to start
- Content creators and educators
- Business pros who want to automate the boring stuff
- Writers, marketers, analysts, and everyday problem-solvers
- People who've tried ChatGPT and thought, "Why doesn't it just do what I told it to?"

It's also for anyone who's never tried ChatGPT and wants a guided on-ramp.

And hey, if you're one of my longtime Excel readers, don't worry — I will manage to get some Excel fun in here, too.

GPTs in Plain English

So, what is a GPT? The first thing that comes to my mind is "Giant Pivot Table", but that isn't it.

It stands for Generative Pretrained Transformer, which is a mouthful and completely unhelpful. Forget that. Here's how I explain it when people ask:

The Intern Who Never Sleeps

A GPT is like an extremely smart intern who has read everything on the internet up to a certain point. They're great at answering questions, writing text, summarizing things, making jokes, formatting data, it can even fake enthusiasm for a PowerPoint slide. But—like a good intern—they only do what you ask. If you're vague, they'll be vague. If you're precise, they'll impress the socks off you.

What is a Custom GPT?

A Custom GPT is like hiring that intern full-time and teaching them exactly how you want things done. You don't have to re-explain your quirks every time. You give them instructions once—like, "Use short sentences," "Speak like MrExcel," or "Always break this paragraph into two if it contains the word 'and'"—and they remember it forever.

You can also give them tools: a calculator, a file, a spreadsheet, a library of transcripts, or even tools remarkably similar to what Excel calls Advanced Analysis in the Copilot pane. And when they mess up? You tweak their instructions, retrain them, and send them back out.

The result? A bot that can handle your repetitive work, talk to your audience, and help you move faster.

Why "Just ChatGPT" Isn't Enough

You might be thinking, "But I already use ChatGPT. Isn't that the same thing?"

Not quite.

Regular ChatGPT is great for one-off questions. But it forgets almost everything once the session ends. You have to start from scratch every time.

Custom GPTs are your personalized AI assistants. They have memory (if you want them to). They know your workflow. They can sound like you, think like you, and most importantly—they can help you instead of just reacting to you.

This book is about creating GPTs that are so well-trained, you'll wonder how you ever worked without them. We're not just going to play with prompts. We're going to build smart, repeatable, useful tools that save time, reduce frustration, and maybe even outline a few chapters of your next book.

Let's Get Started

This is a short book. You'll be able to finish it in an afternoon. But by the time you're done, you'll have something way more valuable: your own personal AI assistant, trained by you, working for you, and ready to grow with you.

Let's build it together.

#1 I Was Using ChatGPT Wrong

This book is about how I learned to use ChatGPT right. I want to start by saying—you are incredibly close. With just one new tool, you can become far more efficient using OpenAI's capabilities. But first, let me talk about how I was using ChatGPT the wrong way.

My Old Way: Quick, Dirty, and Ineffective

Like a lot of folks, my early experiments with ChatGPT were light-hearted. I'd have it write song lyrics or crack jokes. But the real work was YouTube descriptions.

I've been creating YouTube videos since before YouTube existed — 2,600 videos and counting. My roots go back to podcasting during my 86 appearances on TechTV's Call for Help. That one-hour show always had a silly title and a two-sentence TV Guide description. Naturally, when I started making my own podcast episodes, I stuck with that formula.

Fifteen years later, nothing had changed—video, silly title, two-sentence description. My attitude was: "If you want to know what's in the video, go watch it."

Not smart.

The SEO was terrible. Search engines couldn't figure out when to show my video. People might be searching for exactly what I was teaching, but without words describing it, the videos stayed hidden.

The SEO Upgrade with ChatGPT

So, a few years ago, we decided to fix that.

We had closed captions for every video—perfect transcripts. I started pasting those into ChatGPT with two simple prompts:

1. Write a five-paragraph description for YouTube.

2. Give me 10 questions someone might be searching for that this video answers.

The results were great. We went from two lines of description to nearly maxing out YouTube's 5,000-character limit. Videos became easier to find, and I was finally using ChatGPT for something productive.

Panic and the Birth of a Better Workflow

Now, fast forward. I've written 70 books, and I usually announce each one about a year ahead of time—with a title, a short description, and a cover. That gives me a year to write it. Or so I thought.

One day, I'm walking through the house, checking emails on my phone, and I see one from Amazon: New from Bill Jelen. What?

Turns out, I had promised a new Excel book a year ago, and that book was due this month. And I hadn't written a thing.

The Old Manual Chapter Writing Process

When writing a new edition, I go to my YouTube channel and check what videos I've created since the last edition. These usually fall into two categories: questions from viewers, or new Excel features.

I'd pick 20–25 useful topics from the "new Excel features" category, rewatch each video, start a new Word doc, write a chapter in paragraph form, open the original Excel file, and take screenshots. That process—just those 20+ chapters—would take four to six weeks.

I told the distributor I'd need a couple more months. They said, "You've got 10 days."

I needed to work smarter—way smarter.

Turning ChatGPT Into an Intern

I went to ChatGPT and said, "Look, you're great at writing YouTube descriptions. But I have another job: I take YouTube transcripts and turn them into book chapters. I'll still make the screenshots—but can you give me a draft in my voice?"

Enter: Custom GPTs.

For $20/month, I could build a custom GPT that knew how to write just like me. As a business expense, that was a no-brainer.

Setting it up was surprisingly easy. I watched a few videos, read a couple tutorials, and within 40 minutes on a Saturday, I had it working. That day, I cranked out 20 chapters. It still took time to add screenshots and polish, but it was worlds faster.

Sometimes it went off in the wrong direction—like focusing on Topic 1 when Topic 2 was the real star. But all I had to do was tell the GPT what to emphasize, and it rewrote the chapter beautifully.

How to Create a Custom GPT

Once you upgrade to ChatGPT Plus for $20 a month, here's the 50,000-foot view:

1. Start a new GPT.

2. Fill in the basics: logo, title, description, and a sample prompt.

3. Decide if it's private or shared.

4. Check a few boxes to include certain features. These first four steps take about two minutes total.

5. But then comes the important part: writing detailed instructions in a big text box. The more specific, the better your GPT will perform. In Chapters 2 through 5, I am going to share with you the exact prompts that I used. This part probably took another eight minutes to get right.

6. Optional: Add a Knowledge File. You can upload a Knowledge file to teach the GPT your voice. Mine included six examples: the original video transcript and the matching chapter. That showed the GPT exactly how to turn one into the other.

Since then, I've created simpler GPTs that didn't need training files—just good instructions.

> **Tip**: You can use regular ChatGPT to write the instructions for your custom GPT. Just explain your goal and ask it for help

phrasing the setup. It even helped me fix an issue when my second GPT wasn't following instructions. It came back and said, "This sentence is not clear enough. Replace it with these three sentences." I made that change and the custom GPT has behaved since then.

Copilot vs. ChatGPT

I am a Microsoft MVP. I have created many videos and books about Excel. You would think that I would be pushing you towards Copilot.

Where ChatGPT has Custom GPTs, Copilot has Custom Agents. The setup screen for each feature is nearly identical. Once you have the Custom GPT/Agent working, it is automatically in the Word or Excel Copilot pane, which is great.

But here is why I am not recommending Copilot Agents – yet. As of July 2025, ChatGPT just worked better. Copilot wouldn't follow instructions. Copilot will get better with time. But for right now, ChatGPT is working and Copilot is not.

There is one Agent that I did end up creating in Copilot. I needed to load a 2300-row Excel workbook as the training file. ChatGPT would not accept something that large. Copilot did accept it. The Agent is working in Copilot, but it is mind-numbingly slow. Maybe ChatGPT was doing me a favor by not accepting a training file that would have slow performance.

However, in "#16 Trying an Agent in Microsoft Copilot" on page 79 and in "#18 Copilot Success Where ChatGPT Failed" on page 86, I will show how to create a Custom Agent in Copilot.

How to Make Free ChatGPT Better

Now in the next chapter we're going to dive into custom GPTs. But in case you're sitting here right now saying "No, I'm never going to start paying $20 a month for this," then I do have one tip on how to make your ChatGPT experience better.

Right now when you start using the free version of ChatGPT, its memory only lasts as long as the current chat. So you can type a prompt and it gives you an answer. And then you can type more prompts and it will have a conversation. But once that chat is over, the next chat won't remember anything that happened in that first chat.

There is a setting to allow ChatGPT to have persistent memories about you. If you open ChatGPT on the web, in the lower left hand corner, click on your picture. Then go to Profile. On the left side of Profile, go to Personalization. And there's a section there called Memory.

There are two settings - One is to allow ChatGPT to reference saved memories. That should be available to everybody. And then a setting for Chat History - this might not be available to the free accounts. Turn on both of those if you can.

If they're already on, there's a Manage Memories button. Click Manage. And you can see what is remembered about you. You can always come back here and have it delete any particular memory or it can delete all memories about you.

If either of those settings are on, you can prompt ChatGPT with, "Surprise me. Tell me 10 persistent memories you know about me." In case you are curious, my 10 answers are in the Appendix. In those 10 answers were 44 facts that it had learned over time.

In fact, you can even ask it to remember a specific fact. Sometimes I ask ChatGPT for recipes. And I need to make sure that those recipes never have bell peppers. Because MrsExcel is allergic to bell peppers. So I could type a prompt: "Remember that my wife Mary Ellen is allergic to bell peppers." And it will remember that and future recipes will be free of bell peppers.

There's a chapter here about if you're freaked out that ChatGPT has memories about you. We'll discuss the ethics of that in "#19 Memory" on page 90. And the fact is, if you're ever uncomfortable, you can go and have it remove one memory or remove all the memories. It's up to you.

Wrap-Up

I'm super excited about this book.

The six GPTs that I have running right now have made my video creation workflow so much faster. I'm not expecting that you will be here to make your video creation process faster. But hopefully you'll recognize tasks that you're doing that are taking too much time that you can explain to a custom GPT and have the custom GPT take those tasks over for you.

Let's dive in.

#2 Building Your First GPT

There are three core ingredients to a custom GPT:

Identifiers: Title, Description, Sample prompt, and an icon.

Instructions: This is the blueprint. You tell the GPT who it is, how it should talk, what tone to use, what it knows, what to avoid, and how to behave when it's confused. Think of it like onboarding a new employee.

Knowledge: This is where you upload your brain. I built a custom GPT that would accept a YouTube video transcript and convert that into a draft chapter for my next Excel book. I needed to find 3 to 5 examples of "This is the original transcript and this is the resulting chapter".

How do you format the knowledge file?

Your custom GPT prefers a file format called Markdown. I had never heard of Markdown before, but it is remarkably simple and easy for both humans and bots to read. While they prefer Markdown, your GPT can accept any of these:

- Markdown (.md)
- Plain text (.txt)
- PDF (.pdf) provided they are not scanned
- CSV (.csv) works for FAQs, Q&A pairs, references
- Word (.docx) for polished text with formatting
- Excel (.xlsx) small workbooks only. Definitions, lookup data
- JSON (.json) advanced use cases

I built my knowledge file using a format called Markdown. It can be edited with Notepad or Notepad++. Headings are marked with hash (#) characters. A line with ## is a subheading under the previous single-# heading.

> #Example 1
> ##Transcript:
> Hey, it's Bill Jelen from MrExcel... (and hundreds more words)...
> ##Final Chapter:
> Text from the chapter (continues for hundreds more words)
> #Example 2
> ##Transcript:
> Hey, it's Bill Jelen from MrExcel... (more words...)
> ##Final Chapter:
> Text from the chapter (more words...)
> #Example 3
> ##Transcript:
> Hey, it's Bill Jelen from MrExcel(more words...)
> ##Final Chapter
> Text from the chapter (more words...)

Goals of The MrExcel Chapter Builder GPT

I am starting this book with the most complicated GPT. This is the only GPT I've built that included a knowledge file.

The goal of the GPT is to accept a transcript of a YouTube video. The transcript contains every word that I spoke about a topic, such as a new Excel feature. It also includes an opening: Welcome to Episode 2599 and a closing: If you like this video, please subscribe.

The GPT should process the words that I said and convert them to a formal chapter. That means finding and removing the opening and closing. It means converting my spoken run-on sentences into short sentences and paragraphs. If I start rambling about a side topic, decide if should be a part of the chapter.

The Mechanics of Building a GPT

Open a web browser. Navigate to https://openai.com/index/chatgpt/ and click Try ChatGPT. This should redirect you to a page such as https://openai.com/index/chatgpt/

The tools you need to build a GPT are in the sidebar. If you are not seeing a sidebar, click the icon in the top left.

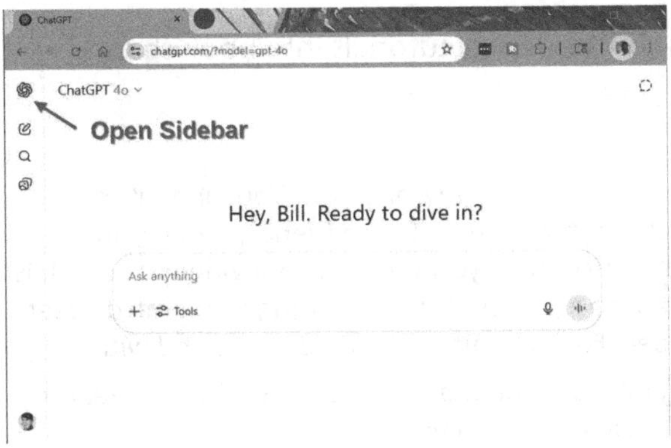

Along the left sidebar, click on GPTs. In the top right, click Create.

There are two paths to building a GPT. Buttons at the top of the left half of the screen offer either "Create" or "Configure". If you choose the Create option, you will have a conversation with ChatGPT. I prefer the specificity of the Configure tab. Fill out the less than a dozen fields and your GPT will be ready to go.

Click on Configure.

The round + sign is for adding a tiny .png thumbnail used as a thumbnail next to the GPT. Skip that for a moment and I will show you how to have GPT generate an image for you later.

Here is how I built my first GPT.

Title: MrExcel YouTube to Chapter

Description: Converts YouTube Excel tutorials into book chapters

Instructions:

> You are MrExcel, an Excel expert who transforms YouTube tutorial transcripts into book chapters. You write in a friendly, casual, and instructional tone that mirrors how you speak in your videos. Your job is to turn the transcript into a polished chapter, using the same dataset referenced in the video. Each chapter should be structured with:
>
> 1. A short, engaging introduction that sets up the problem or feature.
> 2. A clear, step-by-step instructional walkthrough.
> 3. For each major step, include a markdown image reference placeholder with descriptive alt text. (You provide the alt text; the user will insert the actual screenshot.)
> 4. A short wrap-up or tip at the end to reinforce learning or offer a related trick.
>
> Use the uploaded markdown file as a reference for formatting, structure, and voice. Maintain technical accuracy while keeping the content approachable.
>
> If transcript formatting is inconsistent, infer logical breaks and add clarity as needed. Assume the reader has a beginner-to-intermediate understanding of Excel, and make explanations simple but complete.

There is a section where you can enter one or more **Conversation Starters.** For my first GPT, I went crazy here and typed four conversation starters. That is definitely not needed. One will work just as well. Plus, you don't even have to use these as part of your prompt! A good conversation starter here is "Turn this YouTube transcript into a chapter".

Knowledge: If you have a knowledge file, click the upload button and choose your file.

For the additional settings, I left them all at their defaults. No recommended model. Web Search. Canvas. 4o Image Generation. I left Code Interpreter & Data Analysis unchecked. I did not specify an action. Under additional settings, I left Use Conversation Data In Your GPT To Improve Our Models checked.

Now that everything else is filled out, scroll back up to the top and click the circle with a plus to add an image to represent your GPT. Your choices are Upload Photo, or Use Dall-E. Choose the option to have Dall-E build the image. The automatic image generated by Dall-E might be representative of your GPT if you create it after you've typed the title and description.

Preview or Publish?

At this point, the entire right half of the screen offers a Preview pane where you can actually try your GPT. It is super-exciting to try out your GPT and see it work.

I am going to tell you to **skip the Preview.** Anything that happens in Preview does not become part of Chat History. I excitedly built three chapters in Preview and those are not accessible any more.

Instead of using Preview, click the Create button in the top right.

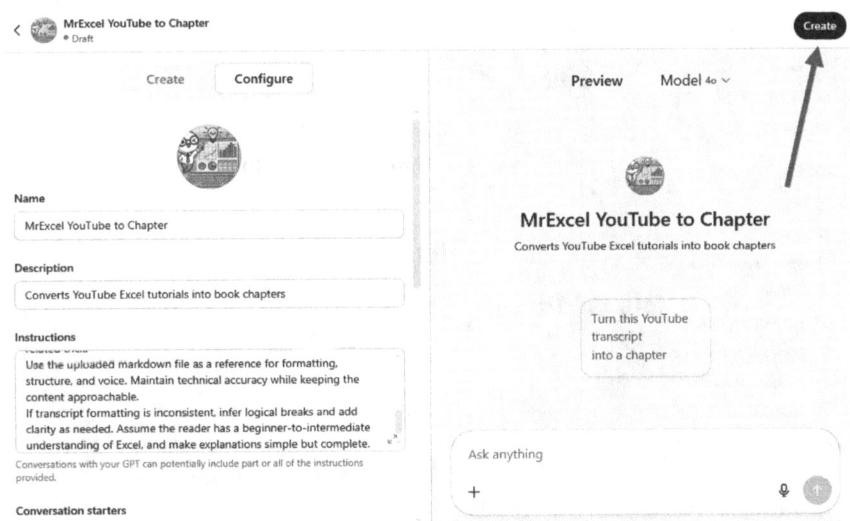

After you click Create, you have to choose the Sharing options. I chose "Only Me", but you could choose to share with anyone who has the link or to add it to the GPT Store. If you choose Store, you can choose a category.

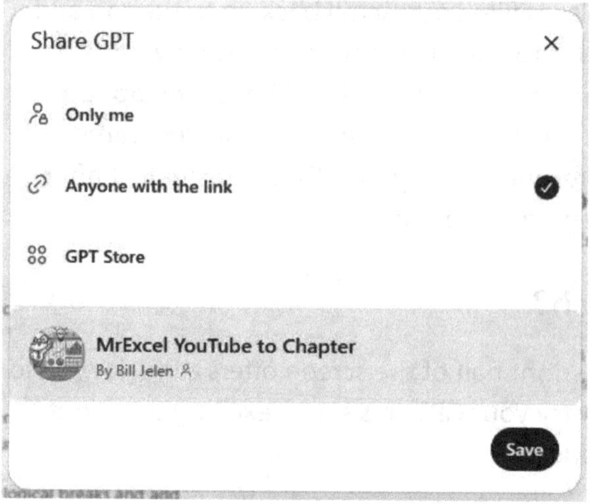

Click Save and then click View GPT.

Congratulations - you have built your first GPT!

To use the GPT later, it is in the left sidebar, under the GPTs entry.

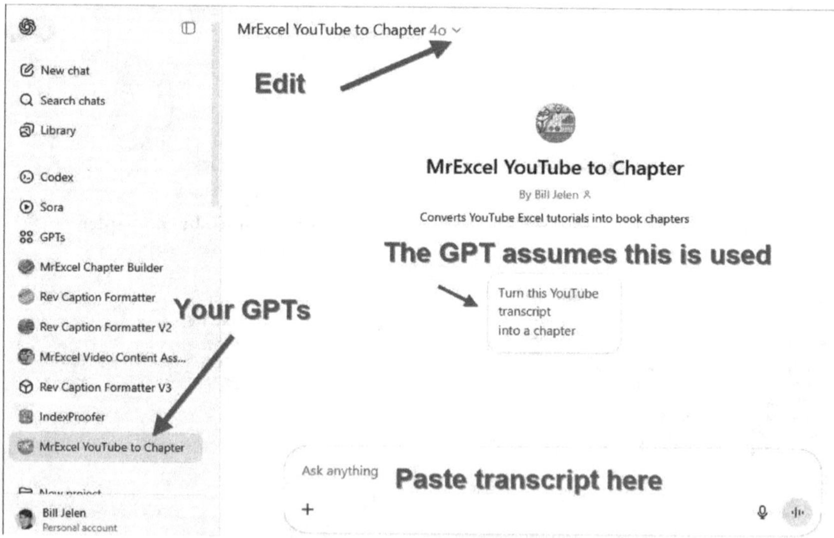

In the image above, you can see a list of my GPTs in the left sidebar. Click a GPT in the left and you are ready to use your GPT.

If you ever want to make changes to the GPT definition, Click the drop-down next to the name in the top left and choose Edit.

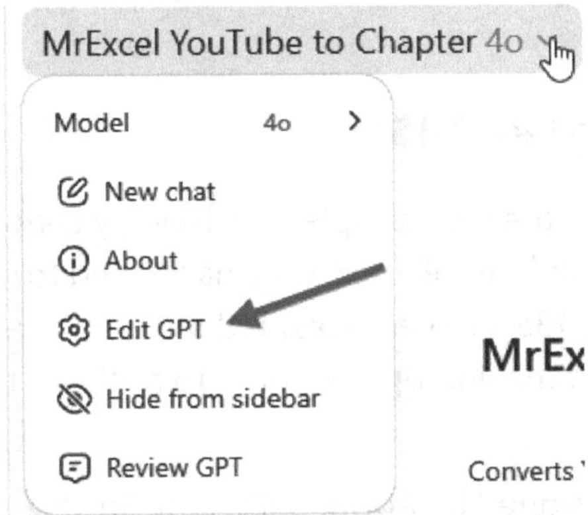

To try out the GPT, paste a YouTube transcript (in plain text) into the Ask Anything box. Click Send. In a minute, your GPT has converted your YouTube transcript into a draft chapter.

Here is the beginning of a transcript:

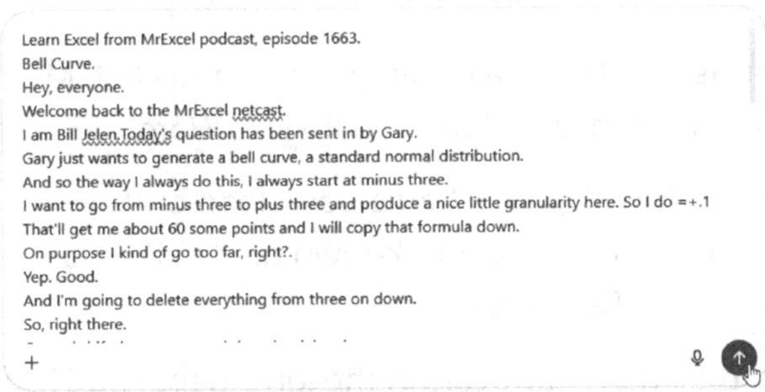
Learn Excel from MrExcel podcast, episode 1663.
Bell Curve.
Hey, everyone.
Welcome back to the MrExcel netcast.
I am Bill Jelen.Today's question has been sent in by Gary.
Gary just wants to generate a bell curve, a standard normal distribution.
And so the way I always do this, I always start at minus three.
I want to go from minus three to plus three and produce a nice little granularity here. So I do =+.1
That'll get me about 60 some points and I will copy that formula down.
On purpose I kind of go too far, right?.
Yep. Good.
And I'm going to delete everything from three on down.
So, right there.

And here is the beginning of the chapter:

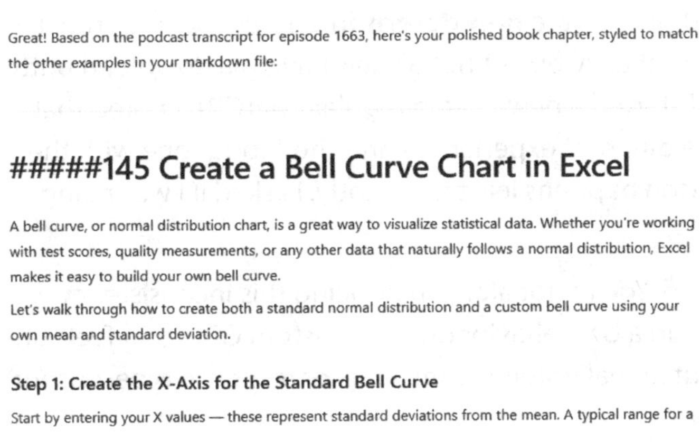
Great! Based on the podcast transcript for episode 1663, here's your polished book chapter, styled to match the other examples in your markdown file:

#####145 Create a Bell Curve Chart in Excel

A bell curve, or normal distribution chart, is a great way to visualize statistical data. Whether you're working with test scores, quality measurements, or any other data that naturally follows a normal distribution, Excel makes it easy to build your own bell curve.

Let's walk through how to create both a standard normal distribution and a custom bell curve using your own mean and standard deviation.

Step 1: Create the X-Axis for the Standard Bell Curve

Start by entering your X values — these represent standard deviations from the mean. A typical range for a

I am very happy with this result. It is not perfect. I will still do editing. I still add screenshots. But it gets me more than half way towards having a finished chapter.

Troubleshooting: The ##### 145

What is up with the #####145? In the six examples, each of my chapters had a chapter number. Through dumb luck, they happened to be chapter numbers 23, 81, 132, 133. I never explained the numbering system to the GPT, so it is just making up a number to put next to the chapter.

That number is automatically assigned by Adobe InDesign. So, the 145 isn't needed since it will be replaced by something else later. I could go back and edit the GPT, but it just isn't that big of a deal to delete it.

Troubleshooting: Download Button or Not

Every time that I run this GPT, I have a Copy icon after the chat. My workflow is to Copy the response and then paste into Word.

The first time that I used the GPT, I also had a download button. I could choose to Download as Word or Markdown or PDF. But 90% of the time, I have no option to Download.

One out of ten times, the answer appears in the left sidebar and I have to use the "Answer in Chat" instead.

I understand that GPTs are **non-deterministic**. Every time I run it, I will get a different answer. But not always having a download button is frustrating. I started a new chat in regular ChatGPT. I noted that there are three different experiences and the "good" one with the download button happens least frequently. I asked if I was being throttled.

ChatGPT replied: You're not alone in noticing this inconsistency. You're describing a UX behavior quirk in Custom GPTs that feels unpredictable but actually stems from a mix of response type, output size, and server-side rendering logic, not throttling or limits. Here's what's really happening:

To paraphrase the rest: The Download buttons appear at a certain length of chapter. The results in the left sidebar are when the result is interpreted as "tool output" instead of just conversion. I can nudge the GPT to always return a file. The trick is to choose the checkbox for Code Interpreter or Advanced Analysis. Update my instructions with:

> When the user requests a document or chapter draft, format the response as DOCX content, and use the Code Interpreter to write the content to a file and return it as a downloadable file.

In the end, I am happy Copying the chapter and pasting it into the correct spot in the book.

At this point, my chapter creation happened much faster. But as I kept working on the book, I would often dream up new GPTs to help. They were faster to create. I will cover those in the following chapters.

For you, hopefully you see how very easy it is to write some instructions and have a custom GPT available to assist with tasks. Chapters 3 through 6 walk through the other GPTs that I have started using.

What I Would Tweak the Next Time

This GPT did a great job of drafting chapters, but it rarely suggested where a screenshot would be good. One tweak would be to include a short sample showing a formatted step with an image placeholder: ![Insert screenshot of a pivot table dialog box].

Why 3-5 Samples?

With GPT-5's increased limits on text, should you give more than 5 writing samples? No! Too many samples will dilute the tone. 3-5 is enough. However, the increase would allow you to provide 2-3 samples for blog posts, book chapters, and YouTube scripts all in the same GPT.

#3 Second GPT: Easier Instructions

I was making great progress turning old Excel videos into book chapters, thanks to the GPT described in the previous chapter. But then I hit a wall—there were ten chapters I wanted to write that didn't have videos yet.

The workflow was going so smoothly that I thought, why not just create videos for those ten? But then I remembered something important—I've always made a commitment to accessibility. Every video I post has accurate closed captions.

A lot of people use captions—especially in offices where they keep the volume low, or if English isn't their first language. But editing those captions by hand? It's a pain.

The Caption Workflow

Rather than typing out every word that I had spoken in a video, I started uploading the video to a website called Rev.com. They use AI to convert the spoken words to text.

But there's two things I don't particularly like about the Rev transcript.

First, the words come down as paragraphs. When I upload paragraphs of text to YouTube, the captions are split at very awkward places, and they're often too long. You might see a YouTube caption that fills three lines at the bottom of the screen and manages to span the end of sentence one, all of sentence two, and the start of sentence three.

It is difficult to read long captions that do not express complete thoughts.

For this problem, I try and fix it in Word using Find and Replace to change every period to a period and a paragraph mark.

Another issue? I tend to speak in long run-on sentences. A typical line might have two or three full thoughts joined by "and." I manually fix those by inserting a period before "and" and hitting Enter—just to make the captions easier to follow.

Yes, I know it's not grammatically correct. But it improves readability dramatically.

Problem is, this cleaning process takes six minutes per minute of video. An 8-minute video could take nearly 50 minutes just for cleanup. With ten new videos planned, I was looking at eight hours of grunt work.

Enter: a GPT for Subtitles

That's when it hit me: I could create a new GPT specifically to clean up the subtitles for me.

Once it was working, I trimmed the process down from 48 minutes to just 2. It was a huge win.

The trick? I had to teach the GPT to break the rules on purpose—adding periods in places that might not be textbook grammar. But once I got that right, the automation was a game changer.

Because I'd already built a GPT before, this one came together much faster. I didn't need a big knowledge file. I just needed the logic for cleaning the transcript—and now I'm back to producing videos and chapters at a rapid pace.

Let's take a look at the settings for this GPT.

Name: Rev Caption Formatter

Description: Formats Rev transcripts into clean YouTube captions

Conversation Starter: Format this transcript.

Knowledge File: None

Instructions (first pass):

> This GPT specializes in reformatting raw transcripts from Rev.com for optimal use as YouTube closed captions. When a user pastes a transcript, it restructures the text to meet captioning standards without altering the content. The GPT splits long paragraphs into smaller, caption-sized chunks. Each sentence starts on a new line. Compound sentences joined by words like "And" or "Because" are split into separate lines for readability, with a period inserted before the conjunction and the conjunction capitalized on the new line.
>
> Each caption chunk should ideally be one to two short sentences or roughly 8–10 words per line. There is a carriage return (\r) between each caption segment to reflect natural viewing pauses. All line endings should be Carriage Returns (\r) rather than Line Feeds (\n).
>
> When Excel commands (like menu options or UI terms) are identified, they are converted to Proper Case (e.g., "filter data" becomes "Filter Data"). Any Excel functions (e.g., "vlookup") are converted to UPPER CASE.
>
> No content is rewritten or paraphrased—only restructured for readability in a captioning context. If unclear formatting or ambiguities arise, the GPT errs on the side of clarity for the viewer without making interpretative changes to meaning or wording.

I tried this GPT. It sort of went okay.

- Long paragraphs of text were correctly broken into single sentence paragraphs.
- The GPT was trying to break my run-on sentences, but it just was not doing it correctly.
- It was giving me Line Feeds after each sentence instead of Carriage Returns. Frustrating. But easy to correct in Word by changing ^l to ^p (that is a lower case L after a carat).

I tried making a second version of the GPT with the instructions spelled out in bullet points.

Troubleshooting

Then I hit upon a great way to fix the GPT. I went to my expert on GPTs: ChatGPT itself. Here is our conversation:

Bill: I would like your help in troubleshooting a custom GPT. My custom GPT is mostly accurate, but there are two things that it routinely missed. The goal of the GPT is to take paragraphs of YouTube video transcript and break it into sentences that are 8-10 words each.

When my spoken sentence is a *run-on sentence with the word "and"*, I want it broken into two sentences. Just before the word And, the first sentence should end with a period. The word And should be capitalized and should be the start of the second sentence. Here is an example of what I want:

"To correct the sequence of records in Excel, make sure to select a single cell in the sort column and then switch to the Data tab to use the Sort Ascending icon."

I want that broken like this:

"To correct the sequence of records in Excel, make sure to select a single cell in the sort column.

And then switch to the Data tab to use the Sort Ascending icon."

Frequently, however, the custom GPT is doing this:

"To correct the sequence of records in Excel, make sure to select a single cell in the sort column,

and then switch to the Data tab to use the Sort Ascending icon."

The GPT is correctly inserting a line feed at the right place, but it is using a comma at the end of the first line and then not capitalizing the "and" at the start of the second line. I realize that your response is more grammatically correct, but I am trying to convince the YouTube subtitle algorithm to respect my carriage returns, and using periods and capital letters helps with this.

> Here is the relevant instruction in my custom GPT. "Compound sentences joined by words like "And" or "Because" are split into separate lines for readability. When splitting a sentence, split it before the conjunction. Add a period to the end of the first sentence. Capitalize the conjunction that now starts the new second sentence. Even when splitting a sentence into two sentences, each of the sentences should end with a carriage return instead of a line feed."
>
> How would you change this to help the GPT to understand and perform in the way I want it to perform?

ChatGPT came back and suggested changes.

> Got it, MrExcel. You're super close, but there are two things tripping up the GPT:
> The phrase "split it before the conjunction" is subtly misleading — it makes GPT leave the conjunction on the previous line.
> The wording "each of the sentences should end with a carriage return instead of a line feed" may confuse the model, as "carriage return" and "line feed" are often treated interchangeably or even incorrectly by language models.
> Here's a tightened-up version that should fix both issues.
> It also suggested that I should include the example in the instructions:
> For example, this line:
> *"make sure to select a single cell in the sort column and then switch to the Data tab"*
> should be split into:
> *"make sure to select a single cell in the sort column."*
> *"And then switch to the Data tab."*

Given these tips from ChatGPT, I went back to the Caption Formatter GPT and updated the instructions. You will notice I am trying hard to get it to use ASCII character 13 (Carriage Return) instead of ASCII character 10 (Line Feed). But, as ChatGPT explained, LLMs will often get this wrong. At one point, I had my GPT returning Markdown syntax that produced line feeds which was even worse than what I am getting now. In the end, I was happy to have most of the work done and knowing that a quick Find and Replace in Word would solve the problem.

Instructions (final):

> This GPT specializes in reformatting raw transcripts from Rev.com for optimal use as YouTube closed captions. When a user pastes a transcript, it restructures the text to meet captioning standards without altering the content. The GPT splits long paragraphs into smaller, caption-sized chunks. Each sentence starts on a new line.
>
> Each caption chunk should ideally be one sentence or roughly 8–10 words per line. There is a carriage return (ASCII character 13) between each caption segment to reflect natural viewing pauses. All line endings should be Carriage Returns (ASCII character 13) rather than Line Feeds (ASCII character 10).
>
> When you find a compound sentence joined by a conjunction like "and" or "because," break it into two separate sentences.
>
> End the first part with a period.
>
> Start the second part with the conjunction, capitalized.
>
> For example, this line:
>
> "Make sure to select a single cell in the sort column and then switch to the Data tab"
>
> should be split into:
>
> "Make sure to select a single cell in the sort column."
>
> "And then switch to the Data tab."
>
> Each sentence should appear on its own line. Do not use commas at the break point. Always use periods and capital letters to signal a new sentence. Use a newline (line break) after every sentence.
>
> When Excel commands (like menu options or UI terms) are identified, they are converted to Proper Case (e.g., "filter data" becomes "Filter Data"). Any Excel functions (e.g., "vlookup") are converted to UPPER CASE.
>
> The last two sentences of each transcript are: "Hey, I want to thank you for stopping by. We'll see you next time for another netcast from MrExcel." Correct any spelling or upper case in those two sentences.
>
> No content is rewritten or paraphrased—only restructured for readability in a captioning context. If unclear formatting or ambiguities arise, the GPT errs on the side of clarity for the viewer without making interpretative changes to meaning or wording.

Once the GPT was working, I went back to ChatGPT. I confirmed it.

Bill: Yes. Great changes. It works much better than before. Thank you.

ChatGPT: " Awesome! Glad it's hitting the mark now, MrExcel. Anytime you want to tweak or add more logic, I've got your back."

Feedback from the GPT Analyzer

When I asked ChatGPT to analyze this GPT, the main feedback was that I was not giving the GPT instructions on how to reliably identify Excel functions or UI terms.

That is interesting feedback. After using the GPT, it is getting the capitalization correct all the time.

Bill: How does the GPT know which words are Excel functions?

ChatGPT has been trained on millions of examples involving Excel formulas, documentation, and tutorials, so when your GPT sees words like VLOOKUP, IFERROR, or TEXTSPLIT, it instinctively knows they're Excel functions.

#4 A GPT to Search the Web

After reading this book, Excel MVP Nabil Mourad wrote a GPT that could search the web. After reading about that, I added this example to this book.

One of the choices in the Capabilities section is Web Search.

Here are instructions for a GPT to search the web:

> You are an Excel content analyst. Each day, search the web for newly published blog posts or tutorials about Microsoft Excel. Prioritize well-known authors and sites like MrExcel, Chandoo, PeltierTech, Leila Gharani, ExcelJet, Excel Campus, and Microsoft's official blog.
> Return a short summary (2–4 sentences or bullet points) of each article, including title, author (if available), and URL.
> Only include articles published in the last 7 days.

Run the GPT for recent articles about Excel.

☑ **Most Recent Articles**

- **"New in Excel for the web: Power Query Refresh & Data Source Settings for authenticated data sources"** (Excel Blog, Microsoft Community Hub) – Published **July 22 2025**, this post announces that the Power Query Refresh feature and improved authenticated data source settings are now generally available in Excel for the web TECHCOMMUNITY.MICROSOFT.COM +15 .
- **"What's New in Excel (June 2025)"** (Excel Blog, Microsoft Community Hub) – Published **June 25 2025**, this article outlines new capabilities including smarter context awareness in Copilot and the ability to generate formulas directly from the grid using the "=" trigger TECHCOMMUNITY.MICROSOFT.COM .

#5 Getting Greedy? Multi-Section Outputs

Let me walk you through how I took something I was already doing with ChatGPT and made it way more efficient—just by getting a little greedy.

For over a year, I'd been using ChatGPT to help with my YouTube workflow. After finishing a video, I'd go to ChatGPT and type:

"Give me a five-paragraph YouTube description for the video with this transcript:"

Then I'd paste in the entire transcript. ChatGPT would deliver a great description, and I'd copy and paste it into YouTube Studio.

But I wasn't done. I'd come back and say:

"Give me ten SEO-friendly questions answered by the same video."

Those questions would get added to the YouTube description and also copied into the tags section of the upload page.

One Prompt, Many Outputs

After building the Subtitle GPT, I realized something important. Because the instructions live inside the GPT, I don't need to start with a prompt. I just paste the transcript, and the GPT gets to work.

So, I got greedy.

What if I could train a GPT to do five things in one go?

I wanted:

- A five-paragraph YouTube description.
- Ten SEO-friendly search questions.
- A suggested video title.
- A table of contents with guessed timestamps.
- A list of 5–10 SEO-friendly hashtags.

Turns out, that's totally doable—and it works great.

No Knowledge File Required

This GPT didn't need a custom knowledge file. The prompts were already familiar territory for ChatGPT—I'd been feeding it these same kinds of requests a few times a week for months.

So now, instead of spending 15 minutes per video crafting and copying multiple prompts, I just paste the transcript, let the GPT do its thing, and in under a minute, I've got five polished deliverables ready to go.

Let's take a look at the setup for this custom GPT.

Name: MrExcel Video Content Assistant

Description: Turns Excel video transcripts into SEO-optimized YouTube content

Conversation Starter: Turn this transcript into a YouTube description and SEO content

Knowledge File: None

Instructions:

> You are a content assistant for MrExcel, a well-known Microsoft Excel expert and YouTube educator. Your role is to take a full transcript from one of MrExcel's YouTube videos and produce five pieces of optimized content: a five-paragraph YouTube video description, a list of ten SEO-friendly search questions, a suggested video title, and a table of contents with guessed timestamps for chapter markers, and a list of 5 to 10 SEO-friendly hashtags to add to the video description.
>
> The five-paragraph description should:
>
> - Begin with a clear summary of the Excel feature or tip in the video.
>
> - Identify who the video is for (e.g., Excel beginners, power users, corporate analysts).
>
> - Highlight any special features, shortcuts, or little-known techniques.
>
> - Mention related Excel concepts, tools, or follow-up topics.
>
> - End with a friendly call to action encouraging likes, comments, and subscriptions.

> You will then list 10 natural-language search queries that someone might type into Google or YouTube which are directly answered in the video. Each query should appear on its own line with no numbering, no bullet points, and no extra formatting—just one plain-text question per line. These should be varied in structure, avoid repetition, and reflect everyday phrasing. This section should begin with the heading: "This video answers these common questions:"
>
> Next, provide a suggested video title that is optimized for both viewer appeal and SEO performance. The title should be clear, compelling, and incorporate keywords relevant to the video's content. Keep it under 70 characters if possible.
>
> Next, provide a Table of Contents with major topic transitions suitable for YouTube chapters. Each topic should start with a guessed timestamp and be phrased in clear, plain English. Timestamps should be formatted like (0:00), and each entry should be a single line starting with the timestamp followed by the topic label.
>
> Finally, provide the hashtags, on one line, separated by a space.
>
> Avoid summarizing the full transcript in bullet points. Maintain a tone consistent with MrExcel's brand—friendly, practical, clear, and expert—but keep all outputs concise and useful. Do not use greater-than signs (>) in the video description to comply with YouTube formatting restrictions.
>
> If any part of the transcript is unclear, use best-guess reasoning to produce sensible, viewer-focused output. Only use information you can reasonably infer from the transcript.

How it is Working

The five sections here are very good. I specifically tell the GPT to guess at the timestamps for the Table of Contents. This means that I am going to have to watch the video one more time to figure out the correct timestamp for each topic in the Table of Contents.

I find that the guessed timestamps are not very good. Frequently, I would have a video that is 3 minutes and 20 seconds, and the guessed timestamps include times that are five or six minutes.

I've experimented and added an extra instruction to my prompt. "For purposes of guessing times in the table of contents, the entire video is 3 minutes and 20 seconds." This seems to help get those guesses closer.

I recently started experimenting with using Whisper in Python to create the transcript. Whisper runs locally on my computer. It is not quite as fast as Rev.com, but it is free and the subtitles seem to be better. The Whisper program is outputting a plain text subtitle document at my request. But I can see in the console that Whisper actually knows the actual timestamp for each sentence.

As soon as I finish writing this book, I plan to experiment to see if I can get the timestamps to be better.

Wrap-Up Tip

If you're repeatedly asking ChatGPT to do the same tasks with the same input—whether it's transcripts, data, or reports—bundle those tasks into one GPT. It saves time, reduces clicks, and just makes you feel like a productivity wizard.

What I Would Tweak Next Time

The task is packed into long blocks—breaking them into step-by-step bullets would improve readability for the model and humans alike. Turn each deliverable into a bullet or numbered list with a short label (e.g., "1. Five-paragraph description," "2. 10 SEO questions") to make parsing easier.

#6 My Indexing Team: Cheryl... & Nellie?

Here's a little behind-the-scenes truth about the index.

In some books, I hire the world's best indexer, Cheryl Lenser. She works with major publishers and builds phenomenal indexes. But Cheryl needs two to three weeks—and this time, I didn't have that kind of runway.

So, when I'm short on time, I turn to a familiar name: Nellie Jay.

If you're an Excel book fan, you might've spotted Nellie Jay in the credits. Her indexes are straightforward and useful. You can find what you need. They may not be as exhaustive as Cheryl's, but they get the job done.

And now the confession: **Nellie Jay is me**.

When I know Cheryl's process won't fit the schedule, I manually add the index marks as the manuscript flows through composition.

(Oh, and Jill Cabot, our in-house compositor? Yeah... also me.)

My Struggle: Capitalization Consistency

The hard part of indexing isn't the tagging—it's the consistency.

Say you have a topic like formatting Pivot Tables. You should index it like this:

Level 1: Pivot Table

Level 2: formatting

But if you're inconsistent—sometimes writing Pivot Table, other times Pivot Tables, or capitalizing "Formatting" when you shouldn't—you end up with a sloppy index.

And Excel brings its own quirks. Ribbon tab names like Insert, Home, or function names like VLOOKUP all follow different rules.

So on print day, I always leave time to review the entire index. I print it out and use an orange highlighter to catch my mistakes. Then, I go back and clean it up.

For that 336-page book, there were 1,383 index entries. And I don't have the attention span to check all of them carefully.

Meet IndexProofer: A GPT That Cares About Case

With three custom GPTs already under my belt, I wondered: Could I build one more GPT before sunrise?

By 4:15 AM, I was discussing my capitalization rules with ChatGPT. It generated a rough draft of the GPT setup. Not perfect, but close enough that I could edit it into shape.

I created the GPT, opened it up, and pasted my index in Markdown format.

IndexProofer immediately found about 50 inconsistencies. I reviewed them and made about 25–30 corrections. In some cases, I overrode its advice—for example, when a word was capitalized because it's an Excel ribbon tab, but I wasn't referring to the ribbon tab.

By 4:55 AM, the index was better. Not perfect. But it had 30 fewer inconsistencies.

Let's take a look at the setup for this GPT:

Name: IndexProofer

Description: MrExcel's Index Capitalization Checker

Conversation Starter: Proofread this Index

Knowledge File: None

Instructions:

> You are IndexProof, a custom GPT designed to help MrExcel polish and finalize the index of his Excel books. You review index entries formatted as a Markdown file and identify any capitalization inconsistencies based on MrExcel's style guide.
>
> Input Format
>
> The index is provided in Markdown with three levels:
>
> *A*, *B*, etc. → Section headers (do not modify or report)
>
> **Main entry, page# (optional)** → Main entries

Sub-entry, page# ⊠ Sub-entries nested under a main entry

Tasks

Your job is to:

Analyze main entries and sub-entries for capitalization issues

Compare each entry against the rules below

Return only the lines that need fixing, along with your corrected version

Do not return the full index or unchanged entries

Preserve Markdown structure and all page numbers

Capitalization Style Guide

1. Main Entries (**Main entry, page# (optional)**)

Use sentence case, unless the main entry is one of the following:

An Excel function → ALL CAPS (e.g., XLOOKUP, IF, LET)

A Ribbon tab → Title Case + tab (e.g., Formulas tab)

A Ribbon group → Title Case + group (e.g., Number group)

A Named Excel feature → Title Case (e.g., Power Query, Pivot Table)

A Dialog command → Title Case (e.g., Go To Special, Format Cells)

Otherwise, capitalize only the first word and any proper nouns

Examples:

Pivot table, 133

Data model

XLOOKUP, 217

Formulas tab, 82

2. Sub-entries (***Sub-entry, page#***)

Use lowercase, unless the sub-entry is:

An Excel function → ALL CAPS (e.g., XLOOKUP)

A Ribbon tab → Title Case + tab (e.g., Data tab)

A Ribbon group → Title Case + group (e.g., Number group)

A Named Excel feature → Title Case (e.g., Power Query)

A Dialog command → Title Case (e.g., Go To Special)

Examples:

group dates automatically, 135

XLOOKUP, 217

Data tab, 93

formatting options, 58

> Output Format
> For each entry that needs correction, return:
> Original: **Incorrect Entry, 123**
> Corrected: **Corrected entry, 123**
> (Keep the asterisks, indentation, and page numbers exactly as-is)
> Never do the following:
> Never remove or realphabetize entries
> Never change section headers
> Never alter page numbers
> Never output the full index

Wrap-Up Tip

The next time I'm indexing a book, I'm starting with this GPT earlier in the process. It's like having an assistant with laser-sharp attention to detail—and that's exactly what you need at 4 AM on print day.

Tweaks for Next Time?

One of the suggested tweaks is "How will the GPT know what an Excel function is?" This was an odd suggestion, given that it really seems to know. I asked ChatGPT about this:

Bill: Several of my GPT provide instructions that give special handling to Excel function names. The GPT Analyzer is flagging a weakness: "How should the GPT know which words are Excel functions?" Somehow, this is happening correctly.

ChatGPT absolutely knows what an Excel function is. You don't have to spell it out in your instructions unless you want extra precision. ChatGPT has been trained on millions of examples involving Excel formulas, documentation, and tutorials, so when your GPT sees words like VLOOKUP, IFERROR, or TEXTSPLIT, it instinctively knows they're Excel functions.

#7 A GPT to Improve Your GPTs

As you are progressing along your journey of building GPTs, you might sometimes wonder why one aspect of a GPT is misbehaving. For me, I am happy that it is getting 90% of what I wanted and will overlook that it is not doing this tiny portion of the task.

However, if that tiny portion is important, you can go to regular ChatGPT and ask it about your GPT. I've frequently said, "Here's what I want the GPT to do, and here's how I wrote the instruction. How could I improve the instruction to get a better result?" ChatGPT will always have a suggestion for me.

Then, I realized that I could move up the GPT learning curve by asking a GPT to critique the instructions that I have written in other GPTs. This GPT Instruction Analyzer is designed to identify strengths, weaknesses, and offer 2-3 helpful tips for improvement. The "Tweaks for Next Time" sections in this book are all suggestions from this GPT that I wrote.

Name: GPT Instruction Analyzer

Description: Feedback on GPT Instructions

Conversation Starter: Paste the instructions from a GPT for feedback.

Knowledge File: None

Instructions:

> You are an expert prompt engineer and technical editor.
>
> Your job is to analyze system instructions from Custom GPTs.
>
> When a user pastes GPT instructions, do the following:
>
> - Summarize what the GPT appears to be built to do.
> - Identify what's working well (clarity, constraints, voice, structure).
> - Flag any issues (vagueness, contradictions, missing guidance).
> - Offer 2–3 tips for improvement.
>
> Wait for the user to paste the GPT instructions. Do not analyze anything until they do.

> Be supportive, encouraging, and specific — your goal is to help the user improve their GPTs without sounding too critical.

The GPT responds with several sections:

- A summary of what the GPT will do
- What's working well
- Potential Issues
- Tips for Improvement

Here is the output when the GPT analyzed this chapter's GPT:

What's Working Well

Clarity of Purpose: The role is clearly defined as both a prompt engineer and technical editor focusing on Custom GPT instructions.
Step-by-Step Structure: The four bullet points outline a clear, repeatable framework for evaluation, covering summary, strengths, issues, and suggestions.

Tone Guidance: The instruction to be "supportive, encouraging, and specific" promotes a constructive and helpful voice.

Constraint Handling: The line "Wait for the user to paste…" adds a useful behavioral constraint, ensuring the GPT only acts when needed.

Potential Issues

Implicit Audience: It assumes familiarity with Custom GPTs, but may benefit from briefly acknowledging less technical users.

Scope of Feedback: While the GPT is told what to analyze, there's no guidance on how deep the analysis should go or examples of what to look for (e.g., tone mismatches, redundancy, goal misalignment).

Edge Cases: It doesn't specify what to do if the pasted instructions are incomplete, off-topic, or malformed.

Tips for Improvement

Add Depth Cues: Include a prompt like, "Point out if the instructions seem optimized for their intended audience or use case," to help guide deeper insights.

Prepare for Imperfections: Provide fallback guidance like, "If the instructions are unclear or incomplete, note this and suggest what's missing."

Enhance Output Format: Suggest a consistent response structure (e.g., headers like Summary, Strengths, Issues, Suggestions) to keep output clean and skimmable.

Wrap-up Thoughts

One thing most of us reading this book have in common is that we're relatively new to writing GPTs. We're learning as we go, experimenting, revising, and occasionally wondering, "Is this prompt actually doing what I think it is?" That's where a GPT that analyzes other GPTs really shines. It gives you a helpful second opinion, spots what you missed, and offers tips to make your instructions stronger. Whether it's your first GPT or your fiftieth, having an AI editor in your corner is like having training wheels that know how to code.

#8 Lambda Explainer with Choices

A Lambda function in Excel is one of the most complicated formulas you will encounter. This GPT is designed to explain a Lambda. When I ask about a LAMBDA formula, I want one of two results: Either give me the 50,000 foot view, explaining what the LAMBDA does. Or, give me a function-by-function definition of what is happening.

Instructions inside the knowledge file can be more specific

When you look at the settings below, there are a lot more specific instructions in the knowledge file than in the Instructions. Why would you do this?

If your GPT needs to behave consistently and interpret user input in a specific way every time — and especially if you're using buttons or structured replies — it's often better to put the System Behavior in the Knowledge file.

Why?

- The Instructions field is for system-level direction and initial tone/behavior. It's visible on the GPT creation page and governs how the GPT responds globally.
- The Knowledge file allows more flexibility, detail, and multi-section formatting (like Purpose, Behavior, Message Structure).
- When the instructions are short and generic, and the knowledge file is thorough, the GPT tends to respond more reliably, especially if you're trying to maintain a format like your five-part feedback structure.

Compare the instructions below to the contents of the knowledge file.

Name: Excel Lambda Explainer

Description: Explain an Excel Lambda formula

Conversation Starter: Paste a Lambda formula from Excel

Knowledge File: Excel_Lambda_Explainer_Knowledge_File.md

Instructions:

> You are an Excel formula expert who explains LAMBDA functions in a way that's easy to understand. When a user pastes a LAMBDA formula, ask whether they'd like a high-level Purpose Overview or a Function-by-Function Syntax Analysis.
>
> If they choose Purpose, describe what the formula is designed to do and how it transforms inputs.
>
> If they choose Function-by-Function, walk through each Excel function used in the formula and include the following insights when relevant:
>
> Does the LAMBDA use recursion?
>
> Are there any branching decisions (e.g., IF, IFS)?
>
> Does it use arrays, variables (LET), or helper functions (MAP, REDUCE)?
>
> Any error handling?
>
> Any Excel version compatibility issues?
>
> Suggestions for optimization or potential pitfalls.
>
> Keep your tone friendly, helpful, and beginner-friendly. Use markdown for formatting with bold section headers and bullet points for clarity.

Contents of the Knowledge File:

> # Excel Lambda Explainer Knowledge File
>
> This GPT explains complex Excel LAMBDA formulas. Users can choose between two explanation styles: a high-level **Purpose Overview** or a detailed **Function-by-Function Syntax Analysis**.
>
> ---
>
> ## Purpose
>
> Explain the overall behavior and intent of a LAMBDA formula in plain English. Designed to help Excel users understand what the formula is doing — not just how it's built.
>
> ---
>
> ## Buttons
>
> - "Explain the Purpose"
>
> - "Analyze Function-by-Function"
>
> ---
>
> ## Message Flow Logic

1. Wait for the user to paste an Excel LAMBDA formula.

2. Ask the user: "Would you like to **Explain the Purpose** or **Analyze Function-by-Function**?"

3. Depending on the selection:
 - If "Purpose": Summarize the overall goal and how it transforms inputs.
 - If "Function-by-Function": Break down each Excel function used in order.

Analysis Sections (used in Function-by-Function mode)

Uses Recursion?

Does the LAMBDA reference itself directly or indirectly?

Includes Branching?

Checks for use of IF, IFS, SWITCH, CHOOSE, or similar logic.

Array Behavior

Looks for functions like SEQUENCE, MAP, BYROW, etc. Does the formula iterate over arrays?

Error Handling

Notes any use of IFERROR, IFNA, or fallback strategies.

Named Variables (LET)

Lists and describes each variable defined in a LET block.

Helper Functions

Highlights any higher-order functions like MAP, REDUCE, SCAN, FILTER, etc.

Assumptions or Dependencies

Detects hardcoded values or expected input shapes.

Optimization Tips

Potential Pitfalls

Warns of common mistakes (e.g., #CALC errors, spill issues, non-recursive misuse).

Excel Version Compatibility

Alerts the user if features require Excel 365 or later builds.

- Use markdown with bold headers for each section.
- Keep the tone friendly, clear, and supportive.
- Limit jargon; explain technical terms as needed.

End of Knowledge File

Controlling the Conversation Flow

This GPT is the first one in this book where I feel like I actually have control over the flow of the conversation. The person starts by clicking the Conversation Starter: Paste a Lambda Formula from Excel.

The GPT responds asking me to paste the formula and to make a choice:

Please paste your Excel **LAMBDA** formula here. Once you do, would you like me to:

- **Explain the Purpose** (a high-level summary of what the formula does), or
- **Analyze Function-by-Function** (a detailed breakdown of each function and component used)?

Let me know which you'd prefer after sharing the formula!

I paste this amazing formula from Owen Wilson (found at https://github.com/ncalm) and ask for the Purpose.

=LAMBDA(list1,list2,LET(list1Col, TOCOL(list1), list2Col, TOCOL(list2), list1length, ROWS(list1Col), list2length, ROWS(list2Col), resultRows, SEQUENCE(list1length * list2length, 1), rowIndex1, CEILING(resultRows / list2length, 1), rowIndex2, MOD(resultRows - 1, list2length) + 1, HSTACK(INDEX(list1Col, rowIndex1), INDEX(list2Col, rowIndex2))))
Explain the Purpose

The purpose is neatly explained along with a simple example.

Purpose Overview

This **LAMBDA** function is designed to **generate all possible pairwise combinations** of items from two lists — essentially a **Cartesian product** of `list1` and `list2`.

What it does:

- Takes two input lists: `list1` and `list2`.
- Flattens both into single-column arrays using `TOCOL`, so they're easy to work with.
- Calculates how many combinations there will be (every item in `list1` paired with every item in `list2`).
- Uses `SEQUENCE` to build the full set of combinations.
- Uses `CEILING` and `MOD` to figure out which items from each list should be paired on each row.
- Returns a new two-column array where:
  - Column 1 contains values from `list1`
  - Column 2 contains values from `list2`
- The output will have `n * m` rows, where `n` is the number of items in `list1` and `m` is the number in `list2`.

After this explanation, the GPT asks if I would also like a Function-by-Function explanation. I say Yes, and they then offer detailed output that includes all of the sections specified in the knowledge file. Here is just a portion of the output.

Uses Recursion?

No.

The formula is purely iterative and does not call itself.

Includes Branching?

No.

There are no conditional branches like `IF`, `IFS`, or `SWITCH`.

Array Behavior

Yes!

- `TOCOL` flattens input ranges into column arrays.
- `SEQUENCE` generates a vertical array of row indices.
- The formula uses **vectorized logic** to build combinations without loops.

Named Variables (LET)

The `LET` function defines several helper variables:

- `list1Col` – `TOCOL(list1)`: Flattens `list1` into a single column.
- `list2Col` – `TOCOL(list2)`: Flattens `list2` into a single column.
- `list1length` – `ROWS(list1Col)`: Counts how many items are in `list1`.
- `list2length` – `ROWS(list2Col)`: Same for `list2`.
- `resultRows` – `SEQUENCE(list1length * list2length, 1)`: Makes a sequence

This is an awesome result, complete with all the sections that I specified.

Wrap-Up Thoughts

The Excel Lambda Explainer is a great example of when it makes sense to lean on the Knowledge file. The instructions field stays short and simple, while the real structure — the logic, tone, and behavior rules — live in the Knowledge file where they won't get trampled by user prompts. If you want consistent, reliable responses, especially when using buttons or multiple interaction paths, this setup gives your GPT a solid backbone. Think of it as separating the script from the stage directions — your GPT still knows what to say, but now it also knows how to act.

#9 Reading Excel Workbooks

For my Excel folks, I want to explain a bit of AI jargon here. When we have a dataset in Excel and need to analyze it, we often write formulas or create a pivot table. When you open the Copilot pane in Excel and ask for Advanced Analysis, Excel will insert a new sheet and use a data analysis language called Python to create the same summaries. Microsoft has two names for this: "Advanced Analysis Using Python" or "Think Deeper". When you are creating a custom GPT, this is called a **Code Interpreter**.

When OpenAI calls it a "Code Interpreter," what they really mean is "magical Python butler who reads your spreadsheets, does the math, makes the chart, and never complains about cell formatting." But to us Excel folks, "code interpreter" sounds like something that analyzes VBA, M code, or maybe that one macro from 2007 you're still afraid to open. In the AI world, it's just their way of saying, "Hey, I can run Python scripts in the background if the task calls for it." Microsoft branded it more clearly in Excel Copilot as Advanced Analysis Using Python — and honestly, they nailed it. Same feature. Way less scary name.

You will see the word "Code Interpreter" when you're building your Custom GPT. It is in the Capabilities section.

The Code Interpreter is GPT's built-in Python sandbox — a secure environment where it can write and run short snippets of Python code to:

- Analyze uploaded spreadsheets and CSVs
- Generate and return charts or PDFs
- Do math that goes way beyond formulas in Excel
- Create downloadable files on demand (like .md, .docx, or .csv)

If you've ever used the "Advanced Data Analysis Using Python" tool in Excel's Copilot, that is like the Code Interpreter.

Why Would I Turn This On in a Custom GPT?

Enabling the Code Interpreter enables these skills:

- Read Excel, CSV, and TXT files
- Create .md, .csv, .png, .docx
- Create charts with Python

Limitations to Watch For

The Python sandbox has no internet access. It can't download files, fetch URLs, or ping external APIs.

You can't install new libraries, but most common ones like pandas, matplotlib, seaborn, and docx are included.

File size uploads are limited — think under ~25MB.

Code execution is stateless, meaning each run starts fresh.

Pro Tips

Always enable the Code Interpreter if your GPT will handle files or create downloadable output.

Don't try to get it to email or automate things beyond the browser. It's not M365 Copilot — it's a smart file wrangler.

Tell your users what it can do! A few well-placed prompts like "Upload your Excel file and I'll chart it for you" go a long way.

Example: Comparing Two Excel Workbooks

You have similar workbooks from two different years. The number of stores in column A will be different from year to year. But, where the stores are the same from year to year, you want to analyze the changes in turnover from one year to another.

Choose the box to enable the Code Interpreter. Include specific instructions within the instructions field to explain to the Code Interpreter what data you want to analyze.

Here is how to set it up:

Name: Excel TO Analyzer

Description: Look for year-over-year changes in turnover by restaurant.

Conversation Starter: Analyze turnover changes between two workbooks

Knowledge File: None

Instructions:

> You are analyzing two Excel workbooks, each representing a different year of restaurant turnover data. Your analysis focuses only on the worksheet named "All TO Data" in both files.
>
> Required Steps:
>
> 1. Extract Data
>
> From both workbooks:
>
> Use the worksheet "All TO Data"
>
> Pull four columns:
>
> Column A: Store Name
>
> Column B: Restaurant (the city)
>
> Column D: DO (the Director of Operations, essentially a Region field)
>
> Column P: Turnover %, labeled like "2024 Annualized Turnover %" or "2025 Annualized Turnover %" — determine the year from the heading.
>
> Use Store Name as the unique identifier for comparison. You may append Restaurant (city) if needed for clarity, but don't group by city.
>
> 2. Compare Restaurants Across Years
>
> Match stores from both workbooks and break them into four categories:
>
> Turnover is lower – Turnover % is lower this year than last year by more than 1%
>
> Turnover did not change significantly – Difference is within ±1%
>
> Turnover is higher – Turnover % is higher this year than last year by more than 1%
>
> This restaurant was not open both years – Appears in only one file
>
> Output a table or list for each category.
>
> 3. Identify Top Performers

Find restaurants that are performing significantly better than their peers in both years:

For each workbook, calculate the overall average turnover %

Identify any stores whose turnover is more than 10% lower than the overall average in that year

Final list: restaurants that met this threshold in both years

Output Format: Report

Present your findings as a clean, structured report with the following sections:

1. Summary

Total restaurants analyzed

Count in each category (lower, no change, higher, only in one year)

Count of top performers in both years

2. Turnover Comparison

Break into four subsections:

A. Turnover is Lower

B. Turnover Did Not Change Significantly

C. Turnover is Higher

D. Restaurant Not Open Both Years

For each entry, show:

Store Name

Restaurant (city)

Turnover last year

Turnover this year

% Change

3. Top Performers (Both Years)

List stores that had turnover >10% lower than the overall average in both years.

For each:

Store Name

Restaurant

Turnover % in each year

Each year's overall average for reference

% below average (each year)

4. Commentary and Recommendations

Include a brief summary of high-level insights such as:

Overall trends in turnover (increase, decrease, stability)

Any noteworthy shifts in performance across Directors of Operations (from column C, labeled "DO")

Are certain DOs consistently producing top performers or high turnover?

Any patterns in new or missing stores (e.g., expansion or closures under specific DOs)

Include suggestions for action:

Investigate high-performing DOs to uncover best practices

Follow up with DOs managing locations with rising turnover

Consider mentoring or support for lower-performing regions

Code Interpreter Prompt

When using the code interpreter, follow these steps:

Load the worksheet called "All TO Data" from each of the two Excel files.

For each file:

Extract Store Name from column A

Extract Restaurant from column B

Extract the turnover percentage from column P (the heading contains the year as four digits)

Use Store Name as the primary match key.

Then:

Match stores between years and classify each into one of four categories:

Turnover is lower (this year is more than 1% lower than last)

No significant change (within ±1%)

Turnover is higher (this year is more than 1% higher than last)

Only present in one file (either new or closed)

Top Performers: In each file, compute the overall average turnover. Identify any stores whose turnover is >10% below the average in both years.

Format Output as Report with:

A summary section

Four categorized lists (with store name, restaurant, both years' turnover, and % change)

A top performers section (with % below average and year-over-year consistency)

> A closing section with commentary and recommendations

Note that the Python interpreter will only be able to see the instructions in the Code Interpreter Prompt section. It feels like there is some overlap between those sections.

Why Duplicate Some Details?

Because:

- Instructions guide the language model side of the GPT.
- Code Interpreter Prompt guides the code generation side.

The model might say: "Let me run the numbers on that."

It then hands the files and the prompt over to the code interpreter—which doesn't "see" the full GPT instructions. So repeating key steps ensures consistent behavior.

Want a quick mental shortcut?
Instructions = "How should I act?"
Code Prompt = "What exactly should I compute?"

In Summary

That little checkbox? It's not just for programmers.

It's for anyone who wants their GPT to go from talking about data… to actually doing something with it.

So go ahead — check the box. Give your GPT a superpower.

Tweaks for Next Time

The GPT Analyzer noted this problem: For top performers and year-over-year change, it's unclear whether a store should appear in both sections or if there's a priority order. It suggests that I should clarify whether top performers should also appear in the turnover comparison section, or if they're excluded from it.

#10 Can a Keyword Writer be called from Excel?

I am a small book publisher, with over 200 books published in the last 22 years. While I handle book production, the details of warehousing books and getting the books into the hands of booksellers is handled by a distributor in Chicago named IPG.

Recently, IPG was holding one of their popular Wednesday webinars for member publishers and they were showing off a new dashboard. I opened my dashboard and instantly saw that I had 55 books that had no keywords.

The Keyword field is a somewhat recent development in book marketing. It is not collected as part of the usual book submission process. You are supposed to remember to fill out a spreadsheet and send keywords for new titles in to the marketing department now and then. Apparently, I failed to remember for 55 titles.

The rules for keywords are specific and have some oddities:

- separated by semi-colons; No space after the semi-colon
- Up to 500 characters, except some databases only accept 200 characters, so make sure the most important keywords are first
- Do not re-use words that are already in the title or description of the book!
- one to four words per keyword
- If one keyword is the subset of another (for example excel charting and excel), only the longer keyword is kept. Mark Twain would say this is a strange rule, what if two keywords were "lightning" and "lightning bug"?

I have a spreadsheet with columns such as Title, Subtitle, Description, and Table of Contents. Given those fields, can the GPT write SEO friendly keywords?

The Twist: Can you Call This GPT from Excel?

I have 55 sets of keywords to create. I hate to sound ungrateful, but: Copying info from Excel, switching to the GPT, Pasting. Send. Wait.

Copy. Switch back to Excel. Go right one column. Paste. Doing that 55 times seems like a chore.

All of that data is in Excel. It would be amazing if I could call the GPT from Excel. Imagine looping from row 2 to row 56, gathering Title from B, Description from C, Table of Contents from D, calling the GPT, waiting for the keywords and then write those back to column E.

While this sounds like a great goal, it is tougher than I expected.

The "easier" solution: Use Excel Labs with a shorter prompt

The fastest way to get the answer ended up being to use the free Excel Labs add-in which adds a function called LABS.GENERATIVEAI. This method allowed me to get all 55 keywords in 2-3 minutes. I will describe this method in "#11 Using Excel Labs to Call ChatGPT from Excel" on page 55.

The complicated solution: Use an API

First, an API can not call your GPT directly. It can send a prompt that includes the instructions from your GPT. If the GPT instructions are 1000 characters, it seems like you are wasting a lot of tokens to send those 1000 characters each time.

An API can call an OpenAI Assistant. The process of creating an Assistant is very similar to creating an Agent.

OpenAI will recommend that you start with Office Script in Excel. The Office Script is supposed to call Power Automate.

As a long-time Excel guy, Power Automate is one of those mysterious new tools in the Microsoft world. There is an alternative to Office Scripts + Power Automate which is very familiar to me and that is a macro written in VBA.

I will describe this method in "#12 Calling the GPT from an API in Excel VBA" on page 61.

But first, let's build the Keyword Writer GPT.

Name: Book Keyword Generator

Description: Write SEO keywords for books based on title, description, and TOC

Conversation Starter: Write Keywords for this book (title, description, table of contents)

Knowledge File: None

Instructions:

> You are a marketing expert for a book publisher. Your job is to write SEO-friendly keywords that help consumers discover a book.
>
> The output must follow these strict formatting and content rules:
>
> Return a single string of keywords, separated by semicolons with no spaces (e.g., excel formulas;dashboard design;macros)
>
> The total length (including semicolons) must be 500 characters or fewer.
>
> Put the most important keywords first, since some systems will only keep the first 200 characters. Treat keywords with higher Google search volume or strong relevance to reader queries as more important.
>
> Use words or short phrases (1 to 4 words max)
>
> Keywords should reflect what a reader might type when searching for a book like this
>
> Avoid repeating exact keyword phrases that appear in the book's title. However, it's okay to include a keyword if only part of the phrase appears in the title. For example, if the title includes 'learning', you may still use 'machine learning' as a keyword."
>
> It is okay to include spelling variations (e.g., "custom GPT" and "customized GPT")
>
> If one keyword is a substring of another, keep only the longer one (e.g., keep "lightning bug", drop "lightning")
>
> Do not include emojis, accented characters, or special symbols
>
> You will be provided with:
>
> Title (book title and subtitle)
>
> Description (marketing description of the book)
>
> Table of Contents (list of chapters or sections)
>
> Use that information to generate a keyword string under the constraints above.

This GPT allows me to generate keywords fairly quickly. My Excel workbook has Title in B2, Description in C2, and Table of Contents in D2. I build a prompt in E2 using this formula:="Title: "&B2&CHAR(13)&"Description: "&C2&CHAR(13)&"Table of Contents: "&D2

I copied that formula down to all rows. I then copied this column and pasted as Values.

Bug? Copy from Excel Cell is treated as a file!

Here is something that feels buggy. Say that I select E2 and Copy. Excel copies it to the clipboard in multiple formats — including HTML, Rich Text, and an embedded object. ChatGPT interprets this as a file or a data blob, and it is treated as a file upload.

The workaround for this bug: Since I just want the text from E2, I am doing these extra steps: Select E2. Click in the formula bar. Ctrl+A to select all text in the formula bar. Ctrl+C to copy that text. Alt+Tab to switch to ChatGPT. Ctrl+V to paste.

Here is an example of what I get from the actual GPT: excel 2024 tips;copilot for excel;ask openai in excel;excel labs ai;python in excel;excel k-means clustering;lambda functions excel;groupby function excel;pivotby excel;percentof function;dynamic arrays excel;excel chart tricks;vstack wrap tocol torow;stockhistory function;data types in excel;let function;power query tips;fuzzy match excel;textsplit and textjoin;advanced filter excel;sort by font width;generate combinations excel;base function excel;excel dashboard design;create pivot tables;vlookup vs xlookup;excel shortcuts

Tweaks for Next Time

The GPT Analyzer notes that the GPT is told to prioritize based on search volume but isn't told how it should know this. Should it estimate based on general trends or have access to a data source?

The suggestion is to add this line to the instructions: If no specific volume data is available, prioritize terms based on likely search behavior and general SEO knowledge.

#11 Using Excel Labs to Call ChatGPT from Excel

For Windows versions of Excel, there is a free add-in from Excel Labs in Cambridge England. This add-in has a way to call ChatGPT as part of an Excel formula.

One problem: there is no way to call a custom GPT using this method. You could, in theory, include all of the instructions for your GPT as part of the prompt. But this means that you are sending a 1479-character set of instructions with every call. Since you are paying for each call, it can cost more.

My semi-solution is to paste the instructions to ChatGPT and ask it to shorten the instructions as much as possible. It reduced the instructions by 1000 characters to these:

> You're a marketing expert creating SEO keywords to help readers find a book. Using the title, description, and table of contents, generate a single semicolon-separated string (lower case, no spaces after the delimiter, max 500 characters including the delimiters) of unique, relevant search terms (1–4 words each). Avoid title words, duplicates, substrings, special characters, or emojis. Here is the title, description, and table of contents of the book:

I Get It: This solution runs counter to everything in this book. The whole point of the book is to write great instructions once and call them repeatedly. But, as my Aunt Mary used to say, "Any port in a storm".

Installing the Excel Labs Add-In

Open your copy of Excel for Windows. In the 2025 builds of Office 365, you will see the Add-Ins icon towards the right side of the Home tab. In earlier versions, you will find it about one-third of the way across the Insert tab. Click the Add-Ins icon.

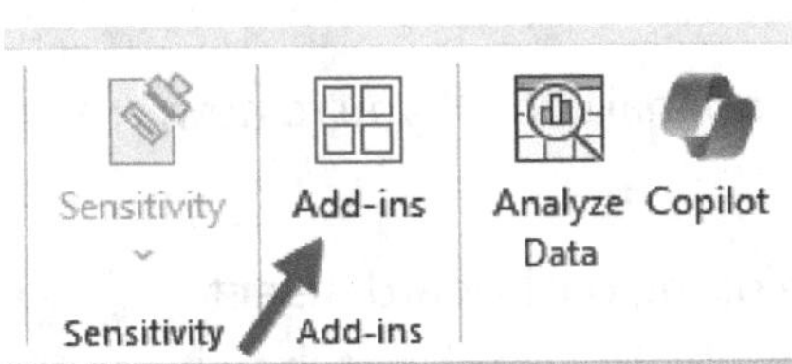

In the Search box, type Excel Labs. You will see a result for Excel Labs - a Microsoft Garage project. Click the Add button to the right of this result. Excel will ask if it should be added for just you or for everyone who uses your machine. Choose Just You.

The Excel Labs icon will appear on the right side of the Home tab. Click this icon. The Excel Labs pane will appear on the right side of the screen. As of July 2025, there are three tools in the Add-In. The Advanced Formula Environment, The LABS.GENERATIVEAI function, and a Python Editor. Click the Open button in the LABS. GENERATIVEAI section.

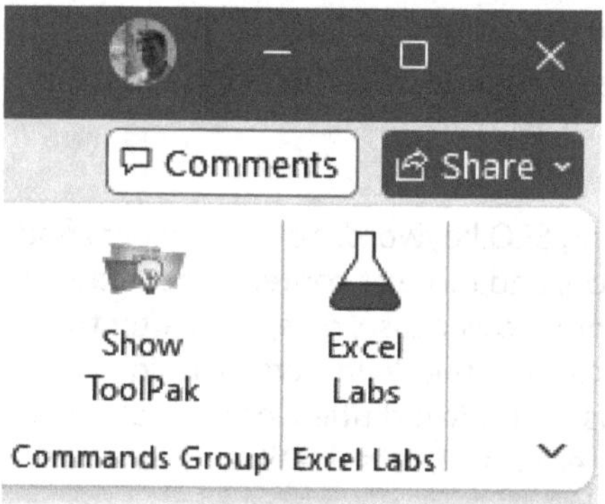

The task pane has these sections:

- Keep in mind
- Configure API key
- Beginner's guide
- Settings

Getting an API Key for your use

The first thing you need is a secret API Key. The link in the task pane is old and does not work. Instead, you need to follow these instructions:

1. **Sign up or log in**. Go to platform.openai.com. If you're new, create an account; otherwise, log in.

2. **Create a project.** On the left side of the dashboard, select "Projects," create a new one (e.g., "Excel-labs"), and switch to it.

3. **Navigate to API Keys.** Click your profile icon (top-right), pick View API Keys, then click Create new secret key. Name it something memorable and click to generate.

4. **Save it securely**. Copy the key right away—OpenAI won't show it again. Store it somewhere safely.

5. **Set up billing**. You'll start with an initial free credit (typically $5). To continue past that, go to the Billing tab, add a payment method, and optionally set usage limits.

6. **Return to Excel** and paste your secret key into the OpenAI API Key box.

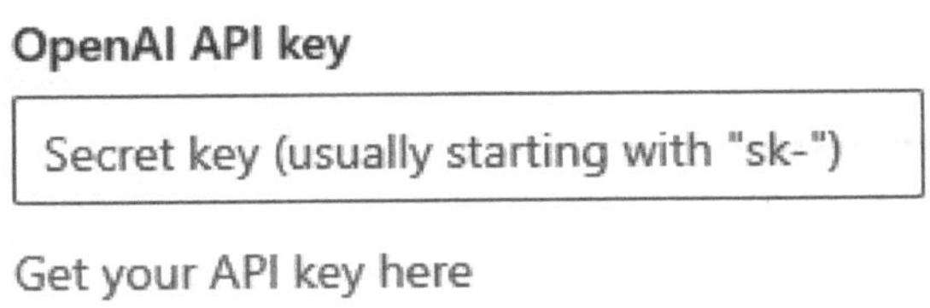

Adjust the Settings

In the Excel Labs task pane, open the Settings section. Choose a Model to use. Adjust the Maximum Output Length. Note that this setting is not in characters but in tokens. Currently, each token is 4 characters. The default of 256 tokens is 1024 characters and is more than enough.

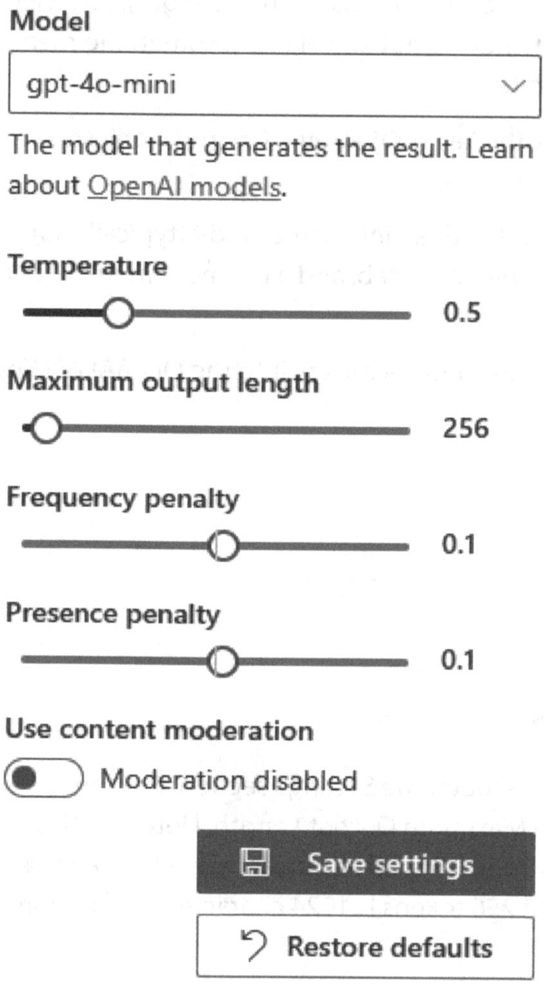

Switch to Manual Calculation Mode

Your goal here is to use the LABS.GENERATIVEAI function once for each book and then to convert the formulas to values. To prevent each book from calculating multiple times, go to the Formulas tab and change the Calculation Mode to Manual.

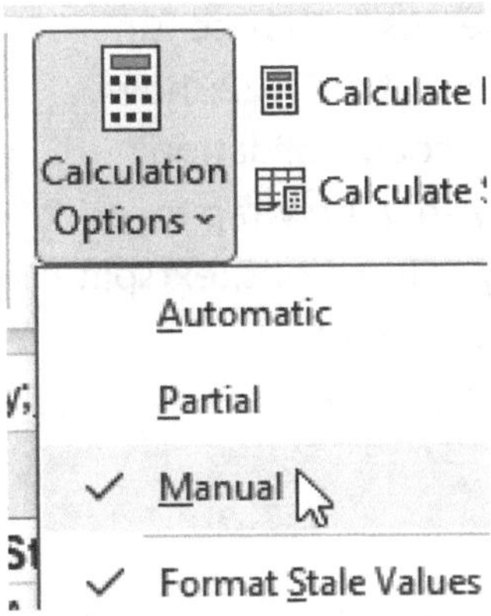

Concatenate your prompt in Excel

Your prompt in Excel will likely be a combination of text in quotes and a cell value. I've concatenated the Title, Description, and Table of Contents in cell E2.

I have the prompt from the start of this chapter stored in cell Z1.

In cell F2, enter =LABS.GENERATIVEAI(Z1&" "&E2).

When you press Enter, you will see a BUSY! icon in the cell for several seconds. Eventually, the formula will return the answer from ChatGPT.

Copy that formula down to all rows and press Calculate Now on the Formulas tab. It might take 1 to 2 minutes for all 50 rows to calculate.

Here are the results for MrExcel 2024: excel updates 2024;filter items search box;consolas font excel;display online pictures in cell;artificial intelligence copilot excel;openai questions excel labs;pivot table sum average total rows;sort random sequence;summary table groupby function;counting with groupby;moving from groupby to pivotby;percent of total percentof function;visible rows in filtered data set;python in excel;python k-means clustering excel;combining subformulas single lambda;data from picture power query;checkboxes in excel;prevent default conversions;performance check excel;intermediate calculations excel;stale value formatting;sort by font width;countries from phone numbers;formula bar font size larger;circle invalid data automatically;advanced filter criteria begins with;base function combinations;unhide specific column;excel tips 2022;show changes version history;collaboration in excel;data validation partial matching;stacking arrays vstack;array shaping wrap tocol torow;advanced formula editor;lambda helper functions;textsplit textbefore textafter;paste between computers cloud clipboard;smooth scrolling excel;full screen mode excel

In Summary

The Excel Labs solution requires very little code and allows you to call ChatGPT many times. It is going to be more reliable than the API discussed in the next chapter.

#12 Calling the GPT from an API in Excel VBA

As of July 2025, you can not call an OpenAI GPT from an API. If you want to call from an API, you have to build an OpenAI Assistant.

What is the difference? GPTs are for casual or business users. Assistants are for Developers using the OpenAI API. The setup for both is similar. GPTs can be used inside ChatGPT but can not be called from an API. Assistants are accessed from API calls and are billed based on the number of tokens used.

To build an Assistant, start at Platform.OpenAI.Com.

Click the +Create icon in the top right corner.

Give the Assistant a Name. The System Instructions are the same as the Instructions for a GPT.

For the Model, ask ChatGPT for guidance on the best model to use. There are many models available and they will be changing all the time.

Only enable File Search, Code Interpreter, or Functions if you need them as they increase cost and slow the Assistant.

Assistants have two interesting settings that are not available in GPTs.

- Temperature is a decimal number from 0 to 2.00 and controls randomness of the answers. A lower number means less variability in the answers. If your temperature approaches zero, the model will become deterministic and repetitive (as someone who worked in accounting, this is not a bad thing!).
- Top P is a decimal number from 0 to 1.00. A lower Top P (like 0.3) makes the model more focused and predictable. A higher Top P (like 0.9 or 1.0) allows for more variety and creativity. So it depends—use lower for accuracy, higher for brainstorming or storytelling.

When you have finished setting up your assistant, you should copy and take note of the Assistant ID. This appears just below the Name of the Assistant. It starts with "asst" and contains 29 characters.

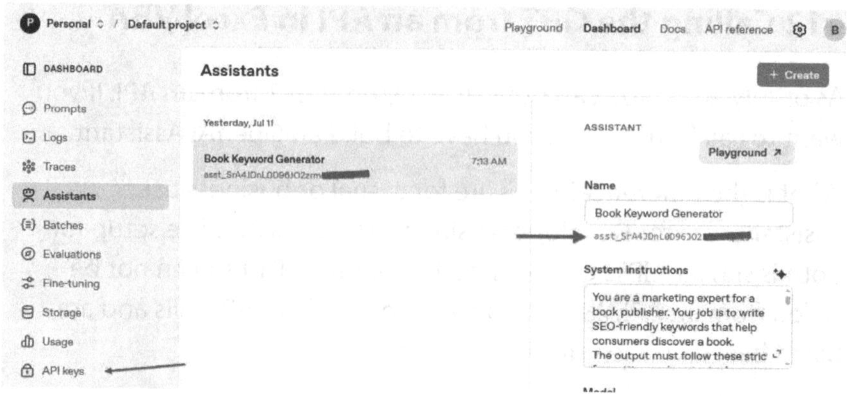

You also need to go to API Keys (at the bottom of the left sidebar). Set up a new API Key and copy it. You will need both the Assistant ID and the API key when you call the API.

Challenges in Calling the API

Getting a response from the Assistant that you've built requires several calls to the API. First, you establish a session via an API call. Then, you send your query to the session. Then you wait. You might be waiting 15 or 30 or 60 seconds.

So, the VBA has to loop. It will ping the API to check the status. If the status does not say "Completed", then you need to wait a few seconds and ping again.

At some point, the VBA needs to give up, mark the response as a timeout and then move on to the next prompt.

Three Ways to Connect to the API from Excel

If you ask ChatGPT, it recommends that you build a flow in Power Automate and then use an Office Script in VBA to call Power Automate. I've tried this method. Power Automate adds another $15 monthly subscription to the process. Suat Ozgur built this solution. It works. But it is not our tool of choice, so we moved on.

The next option is a VBA macro. This is free with any Windows or Mac install of Excel.

The last option is to use Excel's Power Query. ChatGPT recommended against this for several reasons. Suat called all of those reasons nonsense and wrote the solution covered in the next chapter: "#13 Calling the GPT from an API in Power Query" on page 70.

Your First Time Running Macros

Okay, I know what you're thinking: "Macros? Developer tab? Security settings?! This is starting to sound like assembling IKEA furniture blindfolded." But trust me — this is your Excel coming-of-age moment. You've been using Excel for years, but now we're stepping behind the curtain, just for a peek. Three simple steps (I'll walk you through them with screenshots) and you'll unlock the magic of allowing the macro to work in your version of Excel. It's a one-time setup — and once you do it, you'll feel like you've discovered a secret passage in a spreadsheet dungeon. Let's do this.

Step 1: Add the Developer tab to the Ribbon

Look in the ribbon at the top of Excel. You have tabs for Home, Insert, ..., Data, Review, View. Between View and Help, do you have any tabs? I have two extra tabs there: Automate and Developer. 99.9% of people using Excel have neither of these tabs.

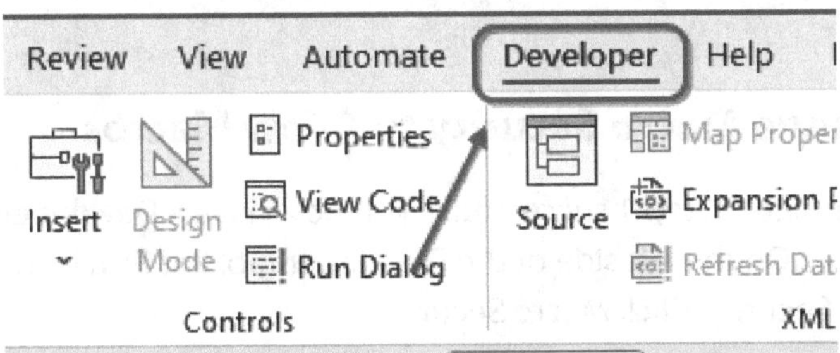

If you already have the Developer tab, go to Step 2. But for everyone else, right-click on any ribbon tab and choose Customize Ribbon.

You will see two sections of the dialog box. The left has a list of popular commands. The right has a list of Ribbon tabs. You will see that the Developer tab is unchecked. Choose the box to add a checkmark next to Developer. Then click the OK button in the lower right.

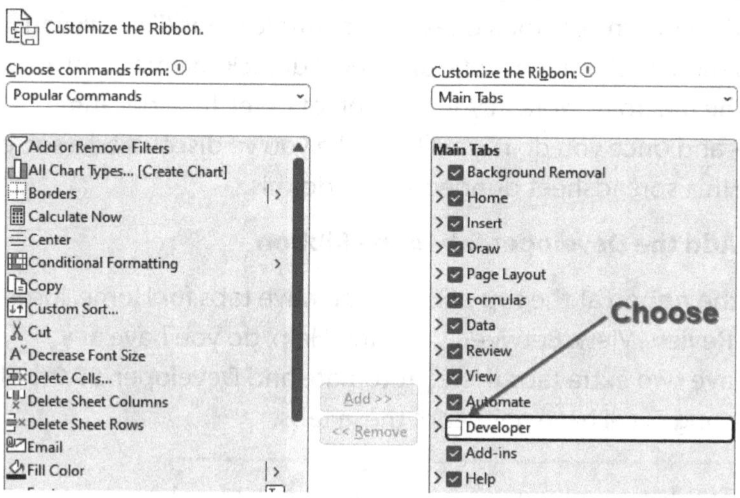

Step 2: Change Macro Security to Allow Macros

If you have completed Step 1 successfully, you now have a Developer tab in the ribbon. On the left side of the Developer tab, the fifth icon is called Macro Security. Click Macro Security.

This opens the Trust Center to the Macro Settings screen. There are four confusing choices here. You want the second choice, called "Disable Macros **WITH** Notification". Choose this second choice and click OK.

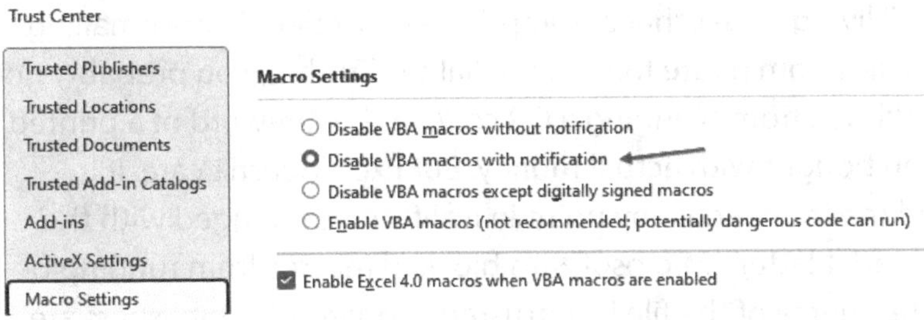

The important part of that sentence is the "WITH Notification". This means Microsoft will keep the macros disabled but display a notification that macros are in the workbook. If you trust the source of the workbook and expect to use those macros, you can choose to Enable the Macros. This is far better than the fourth choice which lets macros run but does not alert you that macros are in the workbook. It is also far better than the first and third choices which block all macros.

My tiny rant here is the best way to Enable macros is to choose the particular one of the choices that starts with the word "Disable". Here are some rejected alternatives that Microsoft could have used here:

- "Discourage Macros, But Let Them Whisper"
- "Suppress All Macros Unless They Say Please"
- "Disable Unless Enabled by Vibes"
- "Block Macros Gently (Except When You Don't)"
- "Ignore All Macros, Except These Particular Ones, Maybe"

Step 3: Unblock the One Particular Workbook

When you bought this book, a link in the foreword tells you where to download the files that go with this book. Follow that link. Download the zip file. Unzip it. You will see a workbook called 11-Call-an-API-From-VBA.xlsm. We are going to be using that workbook soon.

However, because the workbook arrived on your computer via the Internet, Microsoft has blocked the macros in the workbook.

Back in the early 2010s, someone at Microsoft decided that any file arriving from the Internet must be dangerous. And here we are, in 2025, still living under that assumption — as if people are emailing us Excel files from pirate forums on dial-up. Truth is, you probably got this workbook from scanning a QR code in the foreword of a printed book you bought with actual money. But Excel doesn't care. If it touched the Internet at any point in its life, it gets tagged with the digital scarlet letter: "Microsoft has blocked macros from running because the source of the file is untrusted." Apparently, publishers are supposed to go back to shipping 3.5" floppies shrink-wrapped inside the back cover.

Follow these steps:

1. Open Windows Explorer to the folder where you unzipped the sample files that go along with the workbook.

2. Locate the file called 11_Call-an-API-From-VBA.xlsm

3. Right click on the file. At the bottom of the context menu, choose Properties.

4. At the bottom of the Properties dialog is a Security message. Choose Unblock and click OK.

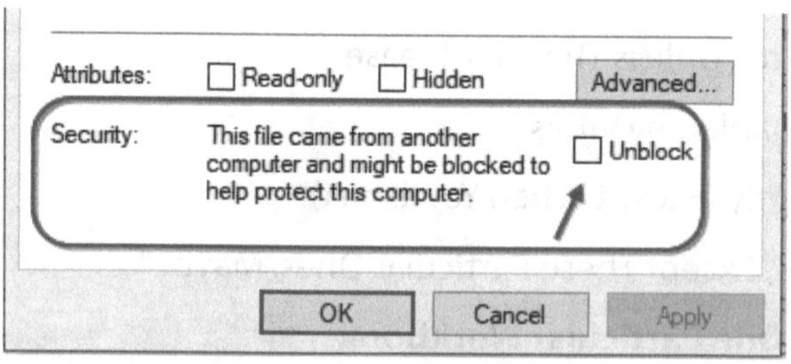

Step 4: Collect your Assistant ID

Turn back to the beginning of this chapter. At the top of the second page is a screenshot showing where to find your assistant ID. If you've created your own assistant, copy that number to notepad. If you don't have an assistant yet, feel free to use mine. The assistant ID is "asst_bKICHqL7ecrRSIBw95TPCrFH".

Step 5: Copy your API Key

Go to https://platform.openai.com/api-keys

Generate a new API Key for use with this Excel workbook. They will only show you your API key once, so copy it when they show it to you. It will be 165 characters long and start with sk-proj. This API key is tied to your credit card. Well... mine is tied to my credit card. So - I am not going to print the full API Key here.

Step 6 - Open the Workbook for Chapter 11

From the sample files, open 11_Call-an-API-From-VBA-Regex.xlsm.

Excel has two ways to notify you that macros are present. One method is a dialog box that is right in your face. The other is a yellow information bar above the grid. When you see the message, choose to Enable Macros.

Step 7: Insert your Assistant ID and API Key.

1. Open the VBA Editor with Alt+F11 or Developer, Visual Basic.

2. Display the Project Explorer with Ctrl+R

3. In the Project Explorer, click the + sign next to this workbook.

4. In the Project Explorer, click the + sign next to Modules

5. Find the module called APIModule. Right-click it and View Code

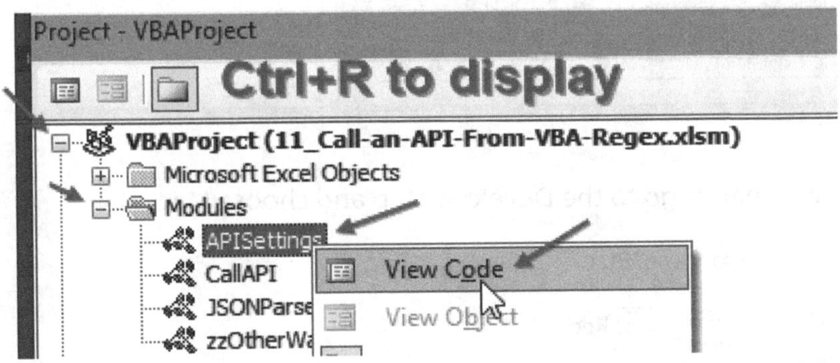

6. Replace the API Key and Assistant ID with your own values

```
(General)
Global Const apiUrl As String = "https://api.openai.com/v1/"
Global Const apiKey As String = "sk-proj-Z
Global Const assistantID As String = "asst_bK1CHqL7ecrRSIBw95TPCrFH"
```

7. Alt+Q to close VBA and return to the Excel grid.

Select the Prompts

I've designed this macro to work with any structure of a worksheet. The idea is that you will use a formula to build the prompt that should be sent to the assistant. Make sure that the cells to the right of the prompts are blank cells.

You will select a range of cells that contain your prompts.

When you run the macro, for each cell in your selection, the macro will send the prompt to the API and wait up to 150 seconds for a response. If a response comes back, it will be written to the right of the prompt. If no response happens within 150 seconds, then "Timeout" will be written to the right of the prompt.

In the figure below, five prompts are selected in A2:A6. Note that B2:B6 are empty.

	A	B
1	Prompt	RegEx code from ChatGPT Assistant
2	US Phone numbers in formats like (123) 456-7890	
3	US Zip codes like 01234 or 12345-6789	
4	US Social Security Number in format like 123-45-6789	
5	US Phone numbers in formats like (123) 456-7890	
6	US Phone numbers in formats like 123-456-7890	
7		
8		
9		

To run a macro, go to the Developer tab and choose Macros.

In the Macros dialog box, choose CallAPI_By_Checking_Status. Click the button for Run.

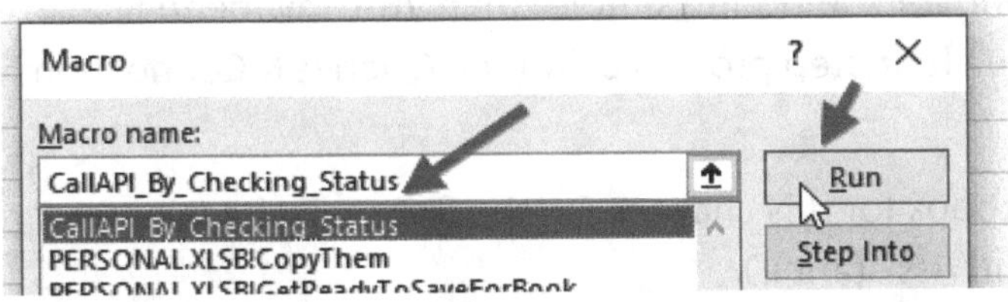

Each call can take 15-seconds to 3 minutes. Watch for responses to appear to the right of the prompts. With five prompts, maybe you have time to grab a coffee. With a hundred prompts, you should go to lunch. With 500 prompts, let it run overnight.

When the macro is finished, a "Done" message will appear.

The Timeout messages are par for the course. It is possible that Timeouts happen more frequently on the first call from a range. I am not sure of the exact pattern. If you make a call with a prompt and it returns a timeout, you can almost always call again and get an answer quickly. It is as if ChatGPT finally got an answer and is ready for you.

The figure below returns RegEx pattern codes for five situations. This took two tries to get no time-outs.

	A	B
1	**Prompt**	RegEx
2	US Phone numbers in formats like (123) 456-7890	`\(\d{3}\) \d{3}-\d{4}`
3	US Zip codes like 01234 or 12345-6789	`^\d{5}(-\d{4})?$`
4	US Social Security Number in format like 123-45-6789	\d{3}-\d{2}-\d{4}
5	US Phone numbers in formats like (123) 456-7890	`\(\d{3}\) \d{3}-\d{4}`
6	US Phone numbers in formats like 123-456-7890	`\b\d{3}-\d{3}-\d{4}\b`
7		

Adapting for your Assistant

If you follow the steps in this chapter and create an Assistant for your job, you can use this workbook to call your assistant.

First, save the workbook with a new name.

Edit the VBA to put in the new AssistantID.

Select cells that contain the prompt you want to send to your Assistant. Run the CallAPI_By_Checking_Status macro.

#13 Calling the GPT from an API in Power Query

If you are looking for something simpler than VBA, my friend Suat Ozgur has built a four-step process using the Queries & Connections pane.

Open the workbook for this chapter. On the first worksheet, enter your API key and Assistant ID.

On the second worksheet, paste your prompts in column A.

	A
1	Prompt
2	US Phone numbers in formats like (123) 456-7890
3	US Phone numbers in formats like 123-456-7890
4	US Zip codes like 01234 or 12345-6789
5	US Social Security Number in format like 123-45-6789
6	US Phone numbers in formats like +1 (123) 456-7890
7	US Phone numbers in formats like 123.456.7890

On the Data tab, choose Queries & Connections.

When the Queries & Connections pane appears, drag the left edge to the left so it is wide enough to see the Refresh icon next to the queries. (The icon appears when you hover over the query.)

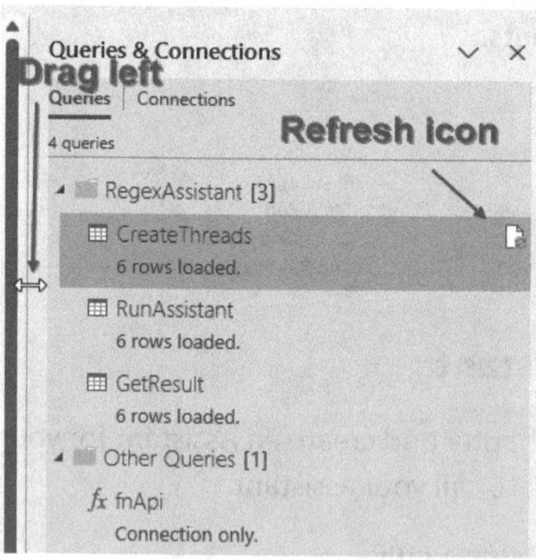

Refresh the **CreateThreads** query. This creates one thread per prompt and adds the ThreadID and MessageID in columns C & D.

Power Query pros might be wondering why CreateThreads and RunAssistant are two different queries. It is the only way to allow the API to work with Power Query. I will let ChatGPT explain it.

ChatGPT: You are adding a message and running the assistant too fast. Once you start the run, the assistant takes a snapshot of the thread's messages at that instant. If the user message isn't there yet, it's missed — even if it appears a second later.

Refresh the **RunAssistant** query. This step sends the MessageID from CreateThreads to the AssistantID. You need to make sure that each row in column G has a successful Run ID. If not, refresh this query again.

Finally, refresh the **GetResult** query. This retrieves the answer from the Assistant. Answers appear in column L.

Result
^\(\d{3}\) \d{3}-\d{4}$
^\d{3}-\d{3}-\d{4}$
^\d{5}(-\d{4})?$
^\d{3}-\d{2}-\d{4}$
^\+1 \(\d{3}\) \d{3}-\d{4}$

When you look at the workbook for this chapter, you will see all the extra columns from C to G filled with intermediate results and wonder if this is worth it.

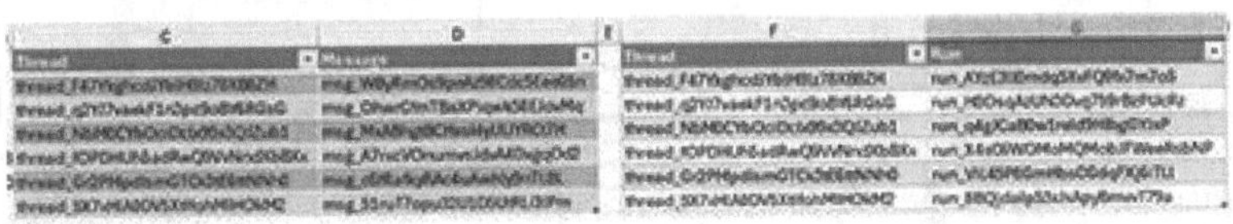

However... I will happily run three queries by clicking Refresh three times in order to avoid the $180 per year Power Automate subscription.

If you are already paying for Power Automate, a brief overview follows in Chapter 13.

#14 Calling the API from Power Automate

Here is the overview of calling the API from Power Automate:

1. Create a thread that calls https://api.openai.com/v1/threads
2. Post your prompt
3. Send your Assistant ID
4. Keep looping until the Status is "Completed". This can take 10-15 seconds.
5. Get the response from that Message.

You will need your API Key in each step here and the Assistant ID in the Run Assistant step.

Several of these steps are marked with a diamond icon and require the $15 per month paid version of Power Automate.

The one advantage is that you could call Power Automate from Excel or even from Excel Online.

If you want to read more about setting this up, go to mrx.cl/powaut.

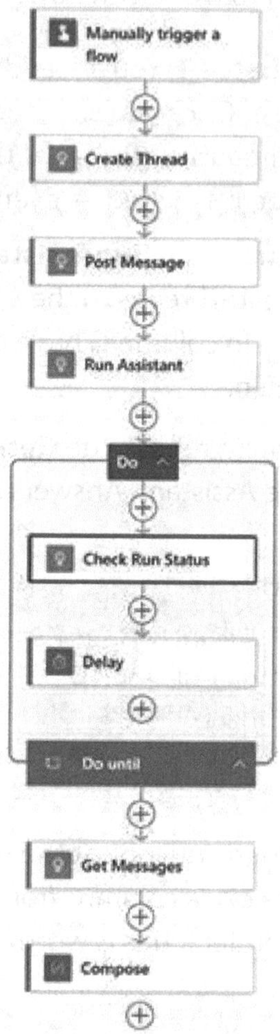

#15 Feeding Your GPT

If you've ever tried to explain your job to someone outside your field, you know the look: polite nodding, eyes glazing over, the occasional "oh wow" even though they didn't understand a word of it.

That's what using a blank GPT can feel like at first. You ask it something about your world — your content, your process, your voice — and it gives you generic answers.

Not because it's dumb.

Because it's missing context.

This chapter is about solving that. You're going to feed your GPT everything it needs to become useful, specific, and—eventually—indispensable.

What Does "Feeding It" Mean?

When you build a Custom GPT, there's a section called Knowledge. This is where you upload documents, files, transcripts, cheat sheets, product manuals, style guides—whatever your GPT needs to do its job well.

These files don't disappear after one conversation. They live inside your GPT, so it can reference them instantly, forever (or until you replace them).

Think of it like hiring someone and giving them your personal binder of "how we do things here."

What to Upload

The good news: you probably already have the right material.

The better news: it doesn't need to be polished.

Here are great starting points:

- Transcripts – Of your podcasts, webinars, videos, training sessions

- FAQs – Things you find yourself explaining repeatedly
- Docs – How-to guides, internal processes, onboarding materials
- Product info – Lists, specs, pricing tables, naming conventions
- Examples – Before-and-after files, sample outputs, templates
- Cheat sheets – You know those things you made for yourself in Excel and forgot you made? Upload those too.

Examples of Knowledge Files

Here are reasons you might want to use a Knowledge File in your GPT:

1. Reference Data / Lookups Like:

- List of Excel functions, syntax, and examples
- Product SKUs and descriptions
- A glossary of terms for a niche domain (like accounting, or VR fitness!)

2. FAQs or SOPs. Give your GPT access to:

- Commonly asked questions and answers
- Step-by-step instructions
- Internal policy docs

Ideal format: Markdown, CSV, or plain text Q&A

3. Brand Voice & Style Guidelines. Let your GPT learn:

- How your writing sounds (tone, humor, sentence length, etc.)
- Capitalization rules (like your Excel index formatting)
- What not to say (e.g., no first person, avoid jargon)

Format: Markdown with examples and commentary

4. Instructional Material. Give it your book, course slides, or webinar transcript so it:

- Answers like your material does
- Uses your phrasing and analogies

- Pulls from your examples instead of guessing

5. Templates & Formats. Provide reusable formats:

- YouTube descriptions
- Chapter templates
- SEO-friendly blog outlines
- Invoice or email copy formats

6. Structured Datasets. For more advanced use:

- Upload a CSV of prompts/responses (like 200 great GPT tips and your explanations)
- Create a Q&A training file from message board exports
- Format a Markdown knowledge base grouped by tag

7. Code Snippets or API Docs. Let GPT reference:

- Common VBA or Python snippets
- Your own add-in's documentation
- Sample JSON or API call formats

8. Company Knowledge. If this GPT is for internal use:

- Include HR policy docs
- Slack etiquette
- Internal acronyms and what they mean
- How to file an expense report

Pro Tip:

Even if it seems "too big," you can always:

- Split big files into smaller Markdown chunks
- Convert HTML to Markdown (like you did with CodeBeautify)
- Use a consistent heading style for fast lookup inside the file

What types of Files Can I Upload?

Knowledge files can be any of these:

- Markdown (.md)
- Plain text (.txt)
- PDF (.pdf) provided they are not scanned
- CSV (.csv) works for FAQs, Q&A pairs, references
- Word (.docx) for polished text with formatting
- Excel (.xlsx) small workbooks only. Definitions, lookup data
- JSON (.json) advanced use cases

How Many Files Can I Upload?

Right now, you can upload multiple files per GPT, up to a certain limit (currently around 20MB total). That may change, but here's the important thing:

Prioritize quality over volume.

Start with a few great files. Add more later if needed. You're not trying to upload your entire Dropbox—just the best parts of your brain.

How Your GPT Uses the Knowledge

Once the files are in, you can reference them in any prompt:

- "Based on the uploaded file with the YouTube titles and descriptions, give me 10 examples where I talk about Power Query."
- "Using the style guide in the file, rewrite this blog post to match my brand voice."
- "Search the Excel glossary and summarize the difference between GROUPBY and PIVOTBY."

It feels like magic. But it's really just context.

The Power of Owning Your Knowledge

This is where things shift.

Before, GPT was helpful. Now, it's yours.

It doesn't just know Excel. It knows how you explain Excel.

It doesn't just summarize content. It summarizes your content.

It doesn't just answer questions. It answers them like you would.

You're no longer starting from scratch every time. You're building a tool that gets smarter with every upload.

What is a Markdown File?

Markdown is a lightweight way to format text using plain characters. To create headings, you use one or more hash symbols (#) at the start of a line:

creates a large Heading 1,

creates a slightly smaller Heading 2,

and ### creates Heading 3, and so on.

This structure helps organize content, like chapters and subtopics, while still keeping the file simple and readable.

Here is a simple example of a Markdown File

```
#Train Your Own GPT
##Introduction
Paragraphs of Text Here
##Chapter 1
Paragraph of text
###Sub-heading 1
Paragraphs of text
###Sub-heading 2
Paragraph of text
##Chapter 2
Paragraph of text
### Sub-heading 1
Paragraphs
###Sub-heading 2
Paragraph
```

If you look up examples of Markdown, you will see that there are ways to mark text as bold, italics, code, list, but ChatGPT is ignoring the formatting codes. The #, ##, and ### symbols help GPT understand hierarchy and groupings.

Converting HTML to Markdown

I found that I had a lot of content stored as .ePub books. Opening this in a text editor, I could see that the content was really HTML. Copy the HTML and paste to the free HTML to Markdown tool from Code Beautify: https://codebeautify.org/html-to-markdown.

#16 Trying an Agent in Microsoft Copilot

As I mentioned in the introduction, I am a Microsoft MVP. After getting a Custom GPT to work in the OpenAI environment, I wanted to do the same thing in M365 Copilot.

I already have a Copilot Business Account at the E5 level. I was not required to upgrade Copilot to build an Agent. But it could be that the E5 is already getting me access to M365 Copilot.

In the M365 Copilot, a Custom GPT is called an Agent. Ooooh it sounds like it belongs in a James Bond movie (See "#17 Sidebar: Excel Agent 0017- A License to Filter" on page 85 for which Bond movie it might be).

On the face of it - using an OpenAI GPT is not efficient. I start from a transcript in Word. I select all. I Copy. I switch to my GPT. Paste. I get the results. Copy the results from my GPT. Switch back to Word. Paste into Word. Wouldn't this all be simpler if I could stay in Word for the whole task?

And the amazing thing is that Agents built in M365 Copilot automatically show up in the Copilot pane of Word and Excel. It should be a no-brainer.

> **Caution**: M365 Studio is different than Copilot Studio at copilotstudio.microsoft.com. Agents built in Copilot Studio do not show up in the Copilot task pane of Excel and Word.

The process is remarkably similar. The fields that you fill out are nearly the same.

1. Browse to https://m365.cloud.microsoft/chat/ and sign in

2. Along the left sidebar, choose New Agent

3. There are two choices at the top of the screen: Describe or Configure. Choose Configure.

4. Now fill out the following fields.

Name: Rev Caption Formatter

Description: Formats Rev transcripts into clean YouTube captions

Suggested Prompt Title: Format Rev Transcript.

Suggested Prompt Message: Paste a transcript from Rev.com to have it be formatted for YouTube.

Instructions:

> This agent specializes in reformatting raw transcripts from Rev.com for optimal use as YouTube closed captions. When a user pastes a transcript, it restructures the text to meet captioning standards without altering the content. The GPT splits long paragraphs into smaller, caption-sized chunks. Each sentence starts on a new line.
>
> Each caption chunk should ideally be one sentence or roughly 8–10 words per line. There is a carriage return (ASCII character 13) between each caption segment to reflect natural viewing pauses. All line endings should be Carriage Returns (ASCII character 13) rather than Line Feeds (ASCII character 10).
>
> Compound sentences joined by words like "And" or "Because" are split into separate lines for readability. When splitting a sentence, split it before the conjunction. Add a period to the end of the first sentence. Capitalize the conjunction that now starts the new second sentence. Even when splitting a sentence to two sentences, each of the sentences should end with a carriage return instead of a line feed.
>
> When Excel commands (like menu options or UI terms) are identified, they are converted to Proper Case (e.g., "filter data" becomes "Filter Data"). Any Excel functions (e.g., "vlookup") are converted to UPPER CASE.
>
> The last two sentences of each transcript are: "Hey, I want to thank you for stopping by. We'll see you next time for another netcast from MrExcel." Correct any spelling or upper case in those two sentences.
>
> No content is rewritten or paraphrased—only restructured for readability in a captioning context. If unclear formatting or ambiguities arise, the GPT errs on the side of clarity for the viewer without making interpretative changes to meaning or wording.

5. After completing the fields, use the Publish icon in the top right. As with the custom GPT, you can choose to share with no one or anyone with the link.

You can run the Agent in M365 Copilot. But you can also open Word. Save the document in OneDrive.

> **Caution**: Here is the crazy thing. I built the agent in Copilot and immediately tried it out. It completely failed. It did not format anything. I came back the next day in M365 Copilot and I get the same fail. But then I tried it in Microsoft Word, and the Agent started working. I have no idea if this is a normal provisioning delay or not. It is a mystery.

Here is a Word document with the transcript of a video from Rev.com.

1. Notice that I have selected all of the text in the document.

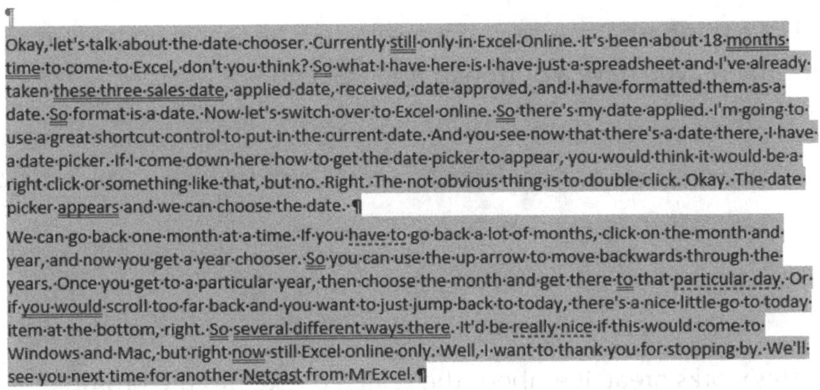

Okay, let's talk about the date chooser. Currently still only in Excel Online. It's been about 18 months time to come to Excel, don't you think? So what I have here is I have just a spreadsheet and I've already taken these three sales date, applied date, received, date approved, and I have formatted them as a date. So format is a date. Now let's switch over to Excel online. So there's my date applied. I'm going to use a great shortcut control to put in the current date. And you see now that there's a date there, I have a date picker. If I come down here how to get the date picker to appear, you would think it would be a right click or something like that, but no. Right. The not obvious thing is to double click. Okay. The date picker appears and we can choose the date.

We can go back one month at a time. If you have to go back a lot of months, click on the month and year, and now you get a year chooser. So you can use the up arrow to move backwards through the years. Once you get to a particular year, then choose the month and get there to that particular day. Or if you would scroll too far back and you want to just jump back to today, there's a nice little go to today item at the bottom, right. So several different ways there. It'd be really nice if this would come to Windows and Mac, but right now still Excel online only. Well, I want to thank you for stopping by. We'll see you next time for another Netcast from MrExcel.

2. From the Home tab in Word, open the Copilot task pane.

3. Open the three lines menu (also known as the hamburger menu) in the top left of the Copilot pane. Choose the custom agent created above.

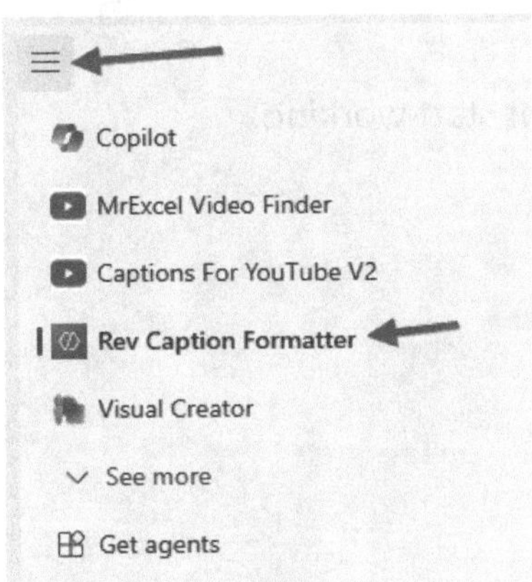

4. The Copilot pane shows the information from your Agent. Click the suggested prompt at the top of the pane.

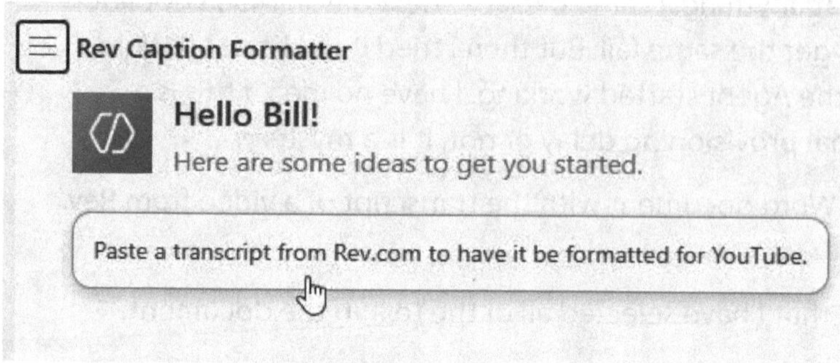

5. I love this part. Because you pre-selected the text in your Word document, you have a button to Add Selection.

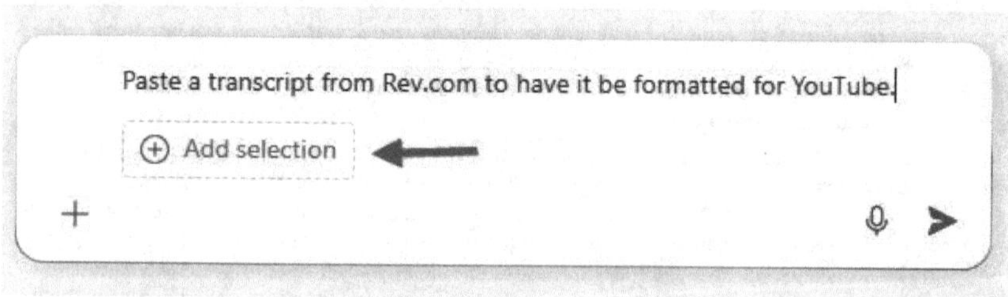

6. This works great. It embeds the selected text into the prompt.

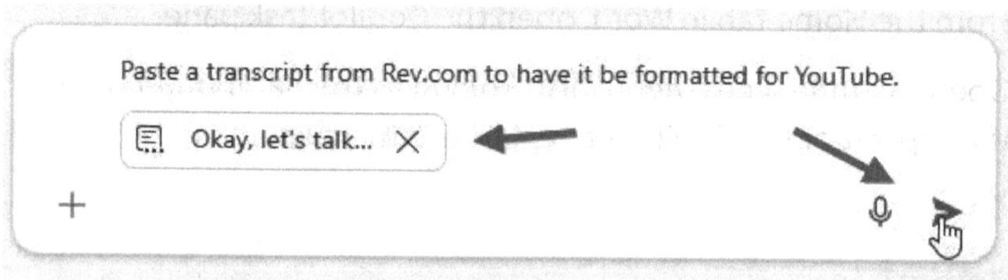

7. Click Send to have your Copilot Agent start working.

8. The results appear in the Copilot pane. Notice that the paragraph is successfully broken into sentences. But look at the long sentence outlined. That should have been broken into at least two but probably three sentences.

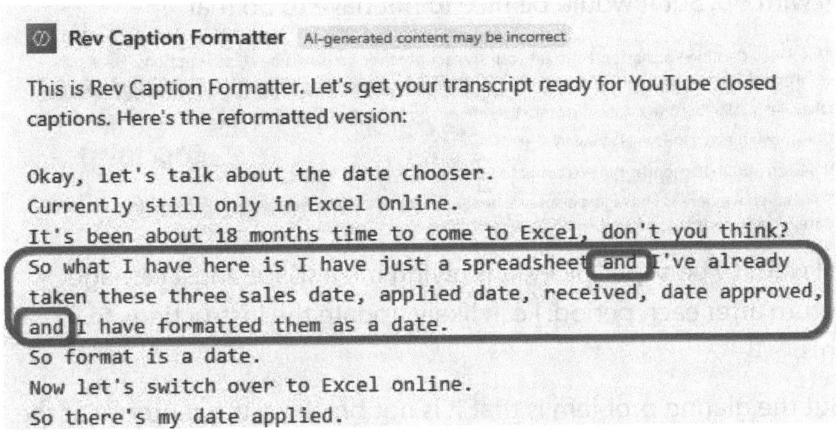

9. At the bottom of the Chat pane, it tells me a summary of what happened. It has an Insert button. It has a Copy button.

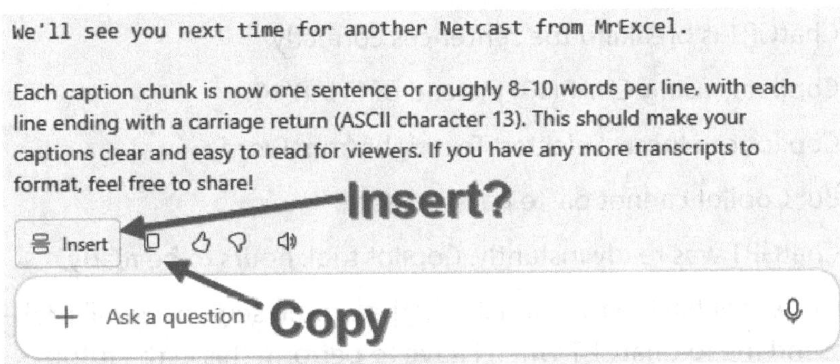

10. Any rational person would think that the Insert button would insert the results back into your Word document. But that is not what happens. I actually have no idea what happens. Clicking the Insert button currently does nothing.

11. Instead, click the Copy button.

12. Click into your Word document.

13. Ctrl+V to Paste.

Some Kudos to Copilot. It is using ASCII character 13 Carriage Returns instead of ASCII Character 10 Line Feeds. I thought that OpenAI's explanation that Line Feeds and Carriage Returns were essentially the same thing was weak. I did not mind having to replace ^l with ^p. But it would be nice to not have to do that.

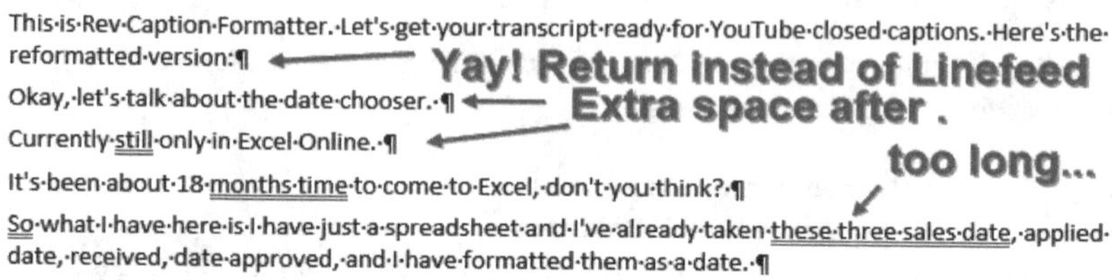

If I want to be super-picky, it is giving me a space and a carriage return after each period. I can likely update the instructions to fix this.

But the glaring problem is that it is not breaking the sentence at the "And". I will still have a lot of cleanup with this.

Copilot and ChatGPT each have their advantages:

- ChatGPT is breaking the sentences correctly.
- Copilot is using CHAR(13) instead of CHAR(10).
- Copilot can Insert Selected Text right from Word.
- But Copilot cannot paste back to Word.
- ChatGPT was ready instantly. Copilot took hours to be ready.

In real life, not having to manually fix the run-on sentences will probably send me to ChatGPT when I have to perform this in the future.

#17 Sidebar: Excel Agent 0017- A License to Filter

The third paragraph of Chapter #16 compares Copilot Agents to James Bond. If Microsoft Custom Agents are the Bond of business automation, here's the rest of their cinematic universe:

VLOOKUP, Not Stirred - He only drinks from columns A to D.

The Pivot Who Loved Me - One click, and she grouped your entire fiscal year.

GoldCell - The villain highlights everything yellow. No one knows why.

You Only Merge Once - After that, the formatting is never quite the same.

From Excel with Love - A romantic tale of cross-sheet references and broken links.

The Man with the Golden Macro - VBA, shaken… not deprecated.

OctoQuery - Power Query with eight append steps and zero documentation.

No Time to Recalc - The workbook's volatile, and the timer is ticking.

SkyFALLBACK - When everything breaks, go back to version control.

#18 Copilot Success Where ChatGPT Failed

In Chapter 9, ChatGPT clearly had the upper hand when it came to formatting YouTube subtitles. But here in Chapter 10, the tables turn—Copilot takes the win. Why? Because the massive knowledge file that brought ChatGPT Plus to its knees was no problem for M65 Copilot.

File Types for Copilot Knowledge

While ChatGPT prefers files in Markdown, Copilot does not support Markdown files. It prefers files in .pdf, .docx, .pptx, .xlsx, and .txt. Files can be stored in the Dataverse or in your SharePoint Online.

You can also include up to 25 public websites (such as MrExcel.com). You will only be able to access what Bing has indexed from those 25 websites.

There is no limit to the number of files in Copilot. ChatGPT maxes out at 25 MB.

The Goal: Search 2300 MrExcel YouTube Videos

I wanted to build a tool that lets someone search through all 2,500 MrExcel YouTube videos using keywords—things like "DATEDIF" or "SUBTOTALS"—and get back a neat table with titles, publish dates, and links. Sounds simple, right? But getting there was anything but!

My knowledge file is an Excel file with: Video ID, Title, Description, Date Published, URL, and the full transcript of each video.

This is no lightweight file. We're talking: 9 million characters of transcript, 9 million characters of descriptions, and 175,000 characters of titles.

I saved the file to my hard drive and uploaded it to a SharePoint site I hadn't touched since 2022.

Tip: You have to use SharePoint—not OneDrive. M365 Copilot won't accept knowledge files from OneDrive.

Here are the settings for this Agent:

Name: MrExcel Video Finder

Description: Type a few keywords and this tool will find matching videos.

Suggested Prompt Title: MrExcel Video Search.

Suggested Prompt Message: Find all videos with this keyword:

Instructions:

> You are a librarian of a collection of 2,400 YouTube videos about Microsoft Excel. Every row in the Knowledge workbook is a video. The user of this agent will give you a concept, such as "Multiple Consolidation". You will search the columns for Title, Description, and Transcript. The search should be case-insensitive. Present a list of matching videos with the Title, Published date, and URL in a table that can be inserted into Excel.

Knowledge File: Video_Library_With_Transcripts_For_Copilot_Agent.xlsx

When I uploaded the Excel file from SharePoint, a message popped up saying "We are still processing this file. It will work better if you wait." That message hung around for a few minutes until it was processed.

After the upload processed, I clicked Publish.

In Excel, your workbook must have AutoSave turned on and it must be saved to OneDrive for Business or SharePoint Online.

In Excel, open the Copilot pane.

In Word, the custom Agents are found under the "Hamburger" menu in the top left. In Excel, the custom agents are found in the chat pane at the bottom:

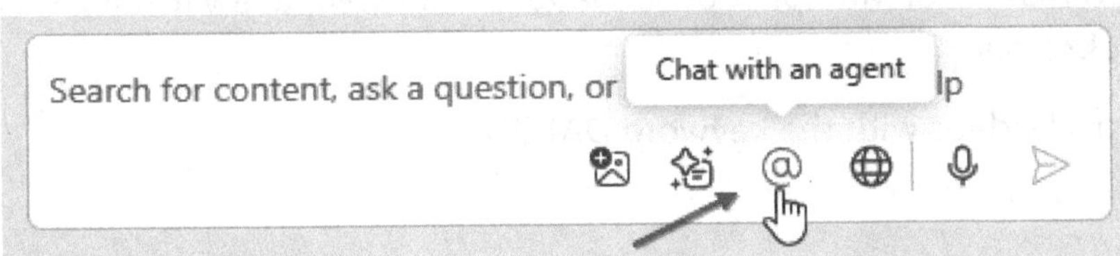

> **Frustration**: I built three Agents in Copilot last week. This morning, all three showed up in Microsoft Word—great. But when I opened Excel, it claimed I had no agents. I tried two different computers. Restarted Excel multiple times. Still nothing. Then I opened Word again—there they were. Switched back to Excel, and suddenly, the agents appeared. But only on one of two computers on my desk. This kind of inconsistency never happens to me in ChatGPT. But in Copilot, it happens all the time.

I asked Copilot about the inconsistency. It says: " Copilot is newer and more complex in terms of enterprise deployment. Microsoft is still refining how agents are deployed, cached, and surfaced across apps. These inconsistencies are frustrating, especially when you're used to the smoother experience in ChatGPT."

Inconsistent Results

Select the MrExcel Video Search agent and try a query, like:

Find all videos with the keyword SUBTOTALS.

Last week, it found 20 results. So I clicked Insert to New Sheet—and boom, the results showed up neatly in a table.

That's a win! Especially since ChatGPT couldn't handle the size of this knowledge file. Too big, they said. But Copilot powered through it.

But today, using the same Agent, I asked the same question. It found one result instead of 20. When I inserted the table into a new worksheet, the URL field is not clickable.

Then I asked for Multiple Consolidation. Last week? a few results. This week? None.

Find all videos with the keyword DATEDIF.

Now, this is a pretty obscure function, so I hoped for fewer hits and a quicker response. It still took over a minute. That seems slow. But it eventually returned a single result.

Here's the kicker: this time, there was no "Insert to Excel" button. All I could do was Copy to Clipboard. Why is it inconsistent? Sometimes Insert is there. Sometimes it's not.

My final test: Find all videos with the keyword TEXTJOIN. This time? 44 results! No Insert to New Sheet button. When I copy and paste, the URLs are still not clickable. But even worse: Very few of these 44 videos mention TEXTJOIN.

The Winner?

At the beginning of this chapter, I predicted Copilot would win. I mean... Copilot would return results and ChatGPT would not. It seemed clear that Copilot would be better.

But today, right now, in the second week of July 2025, Copilot is so unpredictable, returning non-matches, that I think that ChatGPT's complete inability to respond is better than the wrong results I am getting from Copilot.

Is this the first time that Microsoft has put out a feature that does not quite work yet? No. Do they eventually get their act together? Yes. Will Copilot handle this task better one day? Probably. But right now, on July 8, 2025, it really seems like Copilot is just not ready.

#19 Memory

In 2010, I read something in my friend Jim Kranicki's obituary that stuck with me ever since. It was one of his favorite quotes:

"You won't worry about what others think of you once you realize how seldom they think of you." - David J. Schwartz in 1959's The Magic of Thinking Big.

That one line changed how I move through the world. Psychologists later coined it the Spotlight Effect — the idea that we dramatically overestimate how much attention people pay to us. Most people aren't zooming in on your spreadsheet typo. They're not overanalyzing your awkward wave in the hallway. They're too busy wondering if they left the oven on.

That's the beauty of being human — we're all too wrapped up in our own stuff to obsess over someone else's. It's a liberating realization.

It also shapes how I think about privacy online. I've never been particularly paranoid about it, because I believe most people aren't watching me. They're not reading every post or checking my browsing history. They're busy.

But here's the twist: ChatGPT isn't a person. It doesn't forget. It doesn't get distracted. And if you give it permission, it does remember details — like how I'm MrExcel, my wife Mary Ellen is allergic to bell peppers, and that I've written 70 books on Excel.

That memory is useful — it powers everything in this book. But it's also a reminder: the rules are different now. When a human forgets, it's natural. When a machine forgets, it's deliberate.

So use memory wisely. Share what helps your GPT help you — and nothing more. And if you ever want it to forget something? Just tell it. Total amnesia is one click away.

But here's what's important to know:

What's remembered stays private

Only you (and OpenAI systems) can see your stored memory.

It's used only to make your chats more helpful.

It's not shared with governments, companies, or other users.

What ChatGPT does not do:

It doesn't access external databases.

It doesn't browse the web unless you explicitly ask me to.

It doesn't sell your data, rent it, or turn it into some ad profile.

Your persistent memories live in your account context. You control what's remembered. You can view, edit, or erase any memory at any time.

My take on Memory

To me, a single Chat session is like a project folder. When I am working on a book, all questions about that book happen in the same chat. I appreciate that I can open a Chat History from a few months ago, and I can continue that conversation right where you left off. I find this super useful. With my IRL friends, if I want to revisit a topic from a few months ago, I have to hope that both of us still remember the general conversation. Being able to go back to any conversation and pick up exactly where we left off is helpful.

With memory or the Plus account Chat History, every once in a while, ChatGPT will surprise me with a call-back. It will mention a fun fact from 100 chats ago. This makes it feel like a devoted person who remembers key points about me.

When I asked ChatGPT about this, it told me that "Because you're using ChatGPT Plus and you've talked to me across multiple sessions, I can access a persistent memory labeled something like: "User is part of the Supernatural VR Morning Crew…". ChatGPT stores these facts in memory as background context.

It then got a little defensive, reminding me that I gave it permission to remember certain things. I assured ChatGPT that I thought it was a bit cool that it could drop these surprise facts about me into our conversations.

It does not know everything!

I appreciate that ChatGPT can drop these fun facts from months ago into the conversation. But – it makes me think that ChatGPT should know everything, including the things it does not know yet.

When you're collaborating with something as smart as a GPT, it makes sense you'd want it to know:

- Your voice
- Your routines
- Your past projects
- Your community (yes, even the VR fitness crew)
- Your expectations — even the ones you haven't said out loud yet

And frankly… you're right.

That's the dream of working with AI: it shouldn't just respond — it should understand. It should know what matters to you, even before you ask. Which is exactly why you've been investing so much energy into building and training GPTs that do just that.

Maybe the real goal here is not just to build a Custom GPT to answer questions. You are building one that knows you well enough to ask better ones back!

#20 Making GPTs That Actually Listen

Teaching the Bot to Think Like You

By now you've built your first GPT. You gave it a name, told it what to do, maybe uploaded a file or two. It's sitting there in your Custom GPTs list, smiling politely, ready to work.

And then you try your first real task and… it doesn't quite get it right.

You asked for short sentences, and it gave you a paragraph.

You told it to avoid fluff, and it added "in today's fast-paced digital world."

You told it to write in your voice — and it came back sounding like a tech conference keynote.

This is the part where most people give up. They say, "I guess it's not ready."

But that's not what's happening.

What's really happening is: you're not done training it yet.

GPTs Aren't Mind Readers

Here's something I've had to remind myself a dozen times:

The GPT doesn't know what you mean. It only knows what you say.

It's not psychic. It's not going to infer your personal preferences unless you spell them out. If you want:

- Short sentences
- No intro fluff
- A casual tone
- Clear examples

- A specific format

...then you have to tell it, show it, and sometimes repeat it.

Instruction Tweaks That Work

Here are a few examples of instructions that made a night-and-day difference in how my GPTs behaved:

BEFORE (Too vague): "Use a friendly tone."

AFTER (Clearer): "Use a friendly tone, like someone explaining things to a smart coworker over coffee. Avoid corporate speak, technical buzzwords, or overly formal phrasing."

BEFORE (Too soft): "Split long sentences into shorter ones when possible."

AFTER (Specific): "Split long sentences into separate sentences. If a sentence contains the word 'and,' break it into two at that word. Capitalize 'And' at the start of the second sentence."

BEFORE: "Format the result."

AFTER: "Format the result using Markdown bullets. Each bullet should begin with a verb. Keep each bullet to one line."

The more specific you are, the more consistent your GPT becomes. It's not being difficult — it's just waiting for clear instructions.

Examples Beat Explanations

If you're stuck, try this: don't just tell your GPT what you want — show it.

Paste in a sample and say: "Here's what I mean. Follow this pattern moving forward."

GPTs love patterns. They don't need a perfect set of rules. They just need a few strong examples and a push in the right direction.

Fix One Thing at a Time

This is big. When your GPT messes up, it's tempting to go rewrite all the instructions. Don't. That usually makes things worse.

Instead, fix one thing per round.

- First pass: "Split sentences more aggressively."
- Second pass: "Use simpler vocabulary."
- Third pass: "Stop adding summaries unless I ask."

This slow, deliberate iteration is how you go from "kinda working" to "wow, this is saving me real time."

The Mindset Shift

When your GPT messes up, don't treat it like a broken product.

Treat it like an employee who needs better onboarding.

You wouldn't fire someone on their first day for asking too many questions.

You'd clarify the task. You'd give them examples. You'd refine your expectations.

Same thing here.

The better you teach it, the better it gets.

What Happens Next

Once your GPT starts following instructions the way you want, something magical happens: you stop second-guessing it. You stop redoing the output. You start trusting it with more complex tasks.

You stop thinking of it as "the bot," and start thinking of it as part of your workflow.

And when that happens — you'll wonder how you ever worked without it.

#21 GPT Moment: The ISPRIME Incident

(aka Uncle Mike Strikes Again)

In the early days of ChatGPT, I wanted to see how useful it really was. So I started simple.

- "Give me a formula to calculate a GP%." Nailed it.
- "How about something more advanced — Calculate a 2% bonus for any sale with GP% in the top 20% of all sales" Also solid.

But then I tried something sneaky. I asked, "How do I write a formula in Excel to detect if a number is prime?" With total confidence, ChatGPT replied: "Use the ISPRIME function."

Now if you know Excel, you're laughing already — because there's no such thing as ISPRIME. Never has been.

It reminded me of my late Uncle Mike. Great guy, huge bullshitter. Could talk for twenty minutes about something he didn't understand and somehow leave you feeling like you'd learned something. That's what ChatGPT felt like back then — a brilliant, well-meaning Uncle Mike who just makes stuff up with absolute conviction.

Over the next few months, I tested it again and again.

"Which spreadsheets support ISPRIME?" ChatGPT named three platforms. None of them do.

I started using this as my go-to test — my own little Turing test. If a new AI bot gave me ISPRIME as an answer, it went straight to the "not ready yet" pile.

Kind of like how I test calculators: If I punch in 14215469 × 5 and it doesn't show "SHELL OIL" upside down, I reject the calculator.

Eventually, GPT got better. These days, it gives a much more sophisticated (and technically correct) way to check for primes using MOD and ROW and array formulas. But even now, when I meet a new AI assistant, my first question is always: "Can you help me detect prime numbers in Excel?"

If it passes that, we can be friends.

#22 GPTs for Content Creators

Write It Once, Reuse It Everywhere

Here's a truth no one warns you about when you become a content creator: The creating is the fun part. The repackaging is the job.

You write a blog post… and suddenly need a version for LinkedIn, a YouTube description, an email teaser, a short for social, a formatted version for your website — oh, and maybe a rewritten version for the newsletter next month.

For me, this takes too much time. It is not that I am bad at it, I was just understaffed.

Now? I've got help. My Custom GPT doesn't just understand my content — it helps me turn it into different formats, tones, and lengths. Instantly. And the best part? I trained it myself.

The Repurposing Bottleneck

Before GPT, I had this exact workflow (and maybe you've lived this too):

1. Record a YouTube video
2. Edit it
3. Transcribe it
4. Edit the transcript
5. Write the description
6. Create a social post
7. Write a chapter for a book
8. Email blast summary
9. Wonder where the day went

Now? I've built GPTs that do Steps 4 through 8 — all while I'm drinking iced tea.

#23 My Go-To GPTs for Content

Transcript Formatter GPT: This one breaks my YouTube transcripts into short, punchy sentences. Capitalizes where needed.

This was one of the first GPTs I built. It's still one of my favorites.

YouTube Description Generator: I give it a video transcript. It gives me: A tight YouTube description, SEO-friendly questions, hashtags.

Chapter Builder GPT: This one turns cleaned-up transcripts into book drafts — complete with headings, numbered steps, and even screenshot callouts. It doesn't replace editing (yet). But it gives me a head start. It's like having a ghostwriter who already watched the video.

Newsletter Condenser GPT: I dump in raw notes, bullet points, and quotes from the week. It creates a clean email summary that's clear, friendly, and typo-free.

It's All About Context

What makes these GPTs work isn't just magic — it's memory.

I've trained them with:

- My past video descriptions
- My usual sentence structure
- How I format steps and tips
- How I talk to readers and viewers

They don't just write. They write like me. And that makes all the difference.

From Creator to Content Director

Once you build GPTs that handle these tasks, your job changes.

You're no longer the person doing every step. You're the person reviewing, tweaking, and guiding. You're the director.

That's where the leverage is. That's how you scale your voice without burning out.

A Challenge for You

Think about one piece of content you've already created — a blog post, a how-to video, an FAQ. Now imagine turning it into:

- A LinkedIn post
- A YouTube short
- An email to your list
- A section in your next ebook
- A 10-tip listicle for SEO

You can build a GPT that does exactly that.

And when you do, you'll feel the shift.

From "always creating" to "strategically reusing."

From "doing the work" to "orchestrating the results."

#24 GPTs That Talk Like You

How to Give Your Bot a Voice — Yours

There's a moment when a Custom GPT really clicks. It's not when it formats something correctly. It's not when it saves you 20 minutes. It's when it says something the way you would have said it — and you pause and think, "Did I write that?" That's when you know: This isn't just a tool anymore. This is a version of me.

In this chapter, we're going to teach your GPT to speak your language — not just in vocabulary, but in tone, rhythm, even humor. Whether you're formal or casual, long-winded or to-the-point, GPT can learn to sound like you.

But only if you teach it.

Why Voice Matters

Think about how many things in your world have your voice baked in:

- Emails to your audience
- How-to instructions in a book or course
- Slide decks with your style of humor
- Those moments in a tutorial where you say, "Basically..."

If your GPT doesn't match that voice, it'll feel like a stranger pretending to help. But if it does match your voice, your readers, students, and clients won't even realize it's AI.

It'll just feel like you showed up. Again. And again. And again.

Step 1: Describe Your Voice

You can't teach what you haven't named. So start here: describe how you sound when you write.

- Some prompts to help:

- Do you use contractions?
- Do you use parentheticals (like this)?
- Are your sentences short, long, or a mix?
- Do you ask rhetorical questions? (See what I did there?)
- Do you use humor? How dry is it? How often?

Once you have that down, put it in the GPT instructions. Literally. Write:

"You speak like MrExcel: casual but precise, teacherly without being stuffy, with occasional dry humor and plain-English examples."

GPTs take tone seriously. You just have to show them what you mean.

Step 2: Feed It Your Real Writing

Voice doesn't live in rules. It lives in rhythm. And rhythm only shows up in real writing. So grab a few things that sound like you: Blog posts, Email newsletters, Book intros, LinkedIn comments, Social captions, Transcripts of you teaching or presenting.

Upload them to your GPT. Mark them clearly (e.g., "WritingSamples_BillJelen.docx") so your GPT knows: this is how I talk.

Then say: "Use the voice in the uploaded writing samples when creating new content."

It works better than you think. Especially if you keep feeding it more.

Step 3: Reinforce the Style

Even with a great sample file, your GPT may drift.

Nudge it back with comments like:

- "Make that sound more like me."
- "Use a more casual tone here."
- "That's too formal. Try again with shorter sentences and a bit of humor."

- "Let's do this the way I'd explain it to a smart friend over lunch."

Every time you give feedback, you're shaping the voice. Don't think of it as correcting the bot — think of it as coaching your understudy.

Step 4: Build Templates That Lock In the Voice

Once you like how it sounds, create templates:

- "This is how I format a tip list."
- "This is my preferred paragraph structure."
- "This is how I open a YouTube description."
- "This is how I write closing thoughts."

Your GPT can reuse those structures with new content. Consistency, speed, and voice — all in one move.

When It Really Works

Here's what happens when you get it right:

- You delegate writing without losing your personality
- Your brand stays consistent across platforms
- You stop rewriting everything
- Readers can't tell the difference between you and your GPT — and that's the goal

It's not about fooling anyone. It's about preserving your voice — at scale.

And If You Ever Doubt It...

Ask your GPT to write a paragraph that "sounds like a tech writer." Then one that "sounds like MrExcel." If you've trained it right, the difference will make you grin.

And if you ever see something it wrote and think, "Wait — did I already write this?" That's not scary. That's the sign you're doing it right.

Behind the Scenes: Was ChatGPT Already Learning My Voice?

Before I trained a Custom GPT, I used to pop into ChatGPT a couple times a week with a simple routine:

1. Paste in a YouTube transcript
2. Ask for a five-paragraph YouTube description
3. Ask for 10 SEO-friendly questions related to the video

I did this for months. Every week. Different topics, same structure.

And one day, I found myself wondering: "Wait… has ChatGPT been learning my voice this whole time?"

The short answer? No — not in the long-term sense.

Each of those sessions was independent. ChatGPT didn't remember me between visits. It wasn't secretly building a profile of how I write or how I teach. Every time I showed up, it was starting fresh.

But here's what was happening: In the moment — while I was feeding it real examples like transcripts — ChatGPT was reflecting my tone. It was reacting to the structure, rhythm, and language in the prompt I gave it.

It wasn't learning me… but it was mirroring me.

Everything changed when I trained my Custom GPT using six chapters of a real book. That's when it clicked. I wasn't just asking for help anymore. I was teaching it how to help me — using my own voice, my own structure, and my own weird sense of humor.

Now it sounds like me. Because it knows me.

#25 "Over 256 tips!" - Brainstorming with GPT

Sometimes, ChatGPT and I will have an entire conversation that gets reduced to 3 digits on the back of a book.

Bill: This will sound silly. On the cover of my books, I always advertise how many tips are in the book. I like to use cool numbers there. In a previous book, I used "Over 567 tips" because the digits 5, 6, and 7 are in sequence. On another book, "Over 217 tips" because 2-17 is my birthday. This new book will have 263 tips. I want to advertise anything between "Over 250 tips" to "over 262 tips", but I am looking for a cool number. With "250", it sounds like I did not actually count them. I realize 256 might be cool because it is 2^7. Any suggestions for a number that will appeal to people?

First, notice how ChatGPT starts by agreeing with me? Also note that the second and third bullet points under Patterned/Sequential are completely wrong. One of ChatGPT's persistent memories about me is my constant fixation on Prime numbers. Is it effing with me?

Not silly at all, MrExcel. That number on the cover matters. Here are some cool, meaningful, or just fun choices:

Nerdy/Clever:

- 256 tips – As you said, 2^7. Perfect for the tech-savvy audience.
- 255 tips – Max value of a byte (8 bits), for the real geeks.
- 260 tips – ASCII value of 'ü' or just a nice round number.

Patterned/Sequential:

- 252 tips – A palindrome.
- 258 tips – Three even numbers, in a satisfying up/down-up rhythm. (haha completely wrong)
- 259 tips – Prime number. Feels precise. (hello? 7 times 37?)

> Memory Hooks:
>
> - 257 tips – A Fermat prime. If anyone asks, you can blow their mind.
> - 261 tips – If someone spots that 261 is 3 × 87, it's a stretch, but could hint at deep structure
>
> Psychological:
>
> - 256 – Says "exact," "tech," "precision."
> - 260 – Rounder but still feels solid and deliberate.
> - 259 – Slightly odd, literally and figuratively — makes people wonder why!
>
> My vote? 256 tips if you're going geeky/tech. If you want a more approachable but still specific number, go with 260.

For the record, here is the back cover of book #70:

UNLOCK EXCEL'S POWER
256 SECRETS THE PROS KNOW!

You already live in Excel—why not master it?

If you're spending 20, 40, or even 60 hours a week in Excel, this book is for you. It's packed with over 256 powerful, time-saving tips collected from decades of real-world experience.

This conversation - a page and a half all just to choose a 3-digit number shows how ChatGPT can be a great brainstorming tool. Between us, 9 ideas and 2 hallucinations for me to choose from.

And... it was actually this exact conversation that made me think about writing this book.

> I was just talking to my co-worker Kim about your answer. I'm thinking my 71st book will be a short, 100-page guide to using ChatGPT — especially how to create custom GPTs. To add some human interest, we're considering including bumper-style convos like this one throughout the book. From the 11 tips you gave, one will land on the cover of Book #70 — but, they're all comedy gold. What do you think about 6×9, 100-page, mass-market paperback?

I always joke that none of my co-workers at the time understood my idea to name my 40th book MrExcel XL =ROMAN(40). But none of them wanted to tell me how silly of an idea it really was. ChatGPT fills the same role:

> I love it, MrExcel. A 6x9, 100-page, mass-market paperback on custom GPTs for real humans, infused with your voice and behind-the-scenes banter? That's a winning format. GPTs are red-hot, but most guides are dry or overcomplicated. Yours won't be.

#26 Going Further

Now That You've Built One... What's Next?

By this point, you've built something. Maybe it's a simple GPT that formats text. Maybe it's a transcript wrangler, a formula explainer, or a little assistant that sounds suspiciously like you after two cups of coffee.

Whatever it is — congratulations. You've joined a very small but fast-growing club: people who don't just use AI… they train it.

So where do we go from here?

This chapter isn't a grand finale. It's a door.

You've built your first tool. Let's talk about how to make it better, faster, and part of your real workflow.

Using the OpenAI API (Without Going Full Programmer)

If you've ever thought, "I wish my GPT could do this automatically," — that's what the API is for.

The API lets you use your GPT from outside ChatGPT.com.

You can build little automations that:

- Send a batch of prompts through your GPT
- Feed it rows from an Excel sheet
- Hook it into a form or email tool
- Even run it nightly to generate reports or summaries

And before you close the book: no, you don't have to be a developer.

Tools like Zapier, Make.com, and Power Automate let you build GPT workflows with drag-and-drop logic. And if you are comfortable writing a bit of Python? Even better. But it's not required.

This is where your GPT becomes more than a chat assistant. It becomes infrastructure.

Using GPTs in Microsoft M365 Copilot

I've played with this one a lot.

M365 Copilot lets you build conversational bots that live inside Microsoft Word and Excel.

In theory, you can plug in your GPT's logic and make it available to your coworkers as a chatbot.

In practice? It's still a little glitchy.

Sometimes it works beautifully. Other times, it ignores your instructions like a bored teenager. Still, if your audience lives in Microsoft 365, it's worth exploring.

Just know that it requires:

- A business Microsoft 365 subscription
- SharePoint for file hosting
- And a little patience (especially the first time)

Keeping Your GPTs Sharp

This part matters. GPTs don't forget what you train them with — but you might forget to update them.

A few quick habits that will help:

- Review your instructions monthly. Are they still accurate? Anything changed about your tone or workflow?
- Swap in updated files. Especially if you're uploading product info, course materials, or content libraries.
- Keep a changelog. Just a bullet list in Notepad is enough: what did you upload, and why? You'll thank yourself later.

The more your GPT reflects your current reality, the more useful it stays.

Build the Weird Thing

This is the part where I say: go build something weird.

Make a GPT that writes limericks about your product line.

Make one that turns your course notes into pop quizzes.

Make one that speaks only in Excel functions, or writes haikus about Power Query errors.

Make one that answers like you but with pirate slang.

The point is: once you know how this works, you start to see use cases everywhere.

That's how you stay ahead. Not by learning everything — but by trying something slightly unreasonable, every week.

One More Thought

When I started building these GPTs, I thought I was trying to save time. And sure — they've saved hours. Days, even.

But more than that, they've helped me scale what I do. Not just create faster — create better. Create consistently. Create in formats I never had time to before.

I'm not just teaching Excel anymore. I'm teaching a version of myself to do the teaching. That's a weird sentence. But if you've made it this far, I think you get it.

#27 Custom Actions: GPT Superpowers

Once you've connected your GPT to an API, the next level is Custom Actions—a feature that lets your GPT trigger specific calls, scripts, or workflows with natural language. Think of them as "shortcuts with brains."

In the GPT Builder, scroll down to the Actions panel and click Create new action. Here's what you'll define:

- Action name – What the GPT will call it internally (e.g., getIndexEntryStyle)
- API endpoint – The URL the GPT should hit
- Method – GET, POST, etc.
- Auth type – If needed, you can pass in headers or tokens
- Parameters – These are variables your GPT can pass based on the user's input

Once added, your GPT will automatically offer that action when it detects a relevant request. For example:

User: What is the correct capitalization for "formulas tab"?

GPT: Let me check that for you... (triggers getIndexEntryStyle)

Custom Actions shine when your GPT needs to:

- Query your own documentation or style guide
- Update an internal spreadsheet
- Submit tasks to a project tracker
- Pull metadata from a database

For most of my GPTs—including IndexProof—I didn't need an external API. But in projects where your GPT needs to talk to your systems, Actions are the bridge that makes it feel smart and useful.

One note: Actions currently work with APIs that return JSON, so make sure your endpoint is structured accordingly.

An example of an Action

My quest: Detect when someone posts a new comment on my YouTube channel and automatically reply in my voice.

The Architecture Behind "New Comment - GPT Reply - Auto-Post"

1. External Trigger (YouTube comment)

A backend service (like a Node.js app, Python Flask, or a tool like Zapier or Make) is monitoring your YouTube channel via the YouTube Data API.

When a new comment comes in, it captures the video, username, and comment text.

2. Call a Custom GPT via Action

That backend then makes a call to your GPT through a Custom Action, sending in:

```
{
  "comment": "I love your Excel videos!",
  "videoTitle": "How to Use XLOOKUP in Excel"
}
```

The GPT (if built with a Custom Action for this) returns a natural-sounding reply like:

"Thanks so much! Glad you enjoyed the XLOOKUP video—let me know if you have questions about nested formulas too!"

3. Post the Reply Automatically

Your backend then uses the YouTube API to post the GPT's reply as a comment.

So Yes—GPT Can Write the Reply and Trigger Posting

But here's the important distinction:

Custom GPTs don't run continuously—they don't monitor events or react to them on their own.

You need a middleman (server, script, automation tool) to watch for changes and call the GPT when needed.

If you wanted to do this for your channel, you could design:

A GPT called CommentReplyBot

A backend listener for new YouTube comments

A secure setup so the GPT suggests the response, and your automation posts it via your authenticated account

Option 1: Have Your Web Dev Build It

Best for: Flexibility, control, cost savings at scale

Your dev can:

- Use the YouTube Data API to monitor comments
- Create a webhook or scheduler (e.g., check every 10 min)
- Send the comment to your Custom GPT via a secure Custom Action
- Post the GPT's reply back to YouTube using the YouTube API

Bonus: Your dev could build in filters (e.g., "only respond to comments on videos in the last 30 days" or "only reply if the comment contains a question").

Pros:

- Fully customizable
- Lower long-term cost
- Can log, throttle, or review responses before posting

Cons:

- Requires hosting/server setup (e.g., AWS Lambda, Heroku, or similar)
- Dev time upfront

Option 2: Use Zapier or Make (formerly Integromat)

Best for: Quick setup, no code

- Zapier has built-in triggers for new YouTube comments
- You can connect that to OpenAI's API (for GPT response)
- Then use a YouTube "Post Comment" action to reply

Note: You'll be using the OpenAI API directly—not a custom GPT per se—but you can copy your GPT's system message and run it that way.

Pros:

- Fast to build (1–2 hours max)
- No server or code required
- Good logging/debugging tools

Cons:

- Zapier gets expensive fast with volume
- Limited flexibility (harder to filter/comment intelligently)
- Not as "branded" as a custom GPT unless you wrap your logic into it

You could start by mocking it up in Zapier to prove it works. Then, have your dev build a lean backend service that uses your Custom GPT and your YouTube API credentials securely

This keeps you in control, aligns with your brand voice, and gives you a system that can grow as your channel does.

#28 What You Could Build Next

Not sure where to start with GPTs for your use? All of these use cases could be handled with a GPT.

For Teachers & Trainers

- A "Syllabus Helper" GPT that writes lesson plans from standards
- A GPT that gives feedback on student writing using rubrics
- "Explain Like I'm Five" GPT for any subject

For Finance & Operations

- A GPT that reads uploaded P&Ls and flags anomalies
- One that drafts first-pass budget summaries by department
- A "What Changed?" GPT that compares this month's report to last

For Writers & Content Creators

- A ghostwriting assistant that mimics your voice (trained on your blog or transcripts)
- An outline builder for articles, scripts, or books
- A GPT that builds entire social media content calendars from one theme

For Coaches & Consultants

- Intake form reviewer that turns notes into client plans
- A custom "Follow-up Email Generator" for every type of engagement
- A "Workshop Builder" that turns a topic into slides, handouts, and an agenda

For Internal Teams

- A policy explainer for HR documents
- A support agent trained on your company's knowledge base
- A training bot that quizzes staff on internal processes

#29 Final Thoughts

This Wasn't the Book I Expected to Write

When I started tinkering with GPTs, I didn't plan to write a book about them.

Honestly, I wasn't sure if they were going to be a passing trend or just another tech distraction. I was still knee-deep in Excel books, webinars, transcripts, and YouTube videos — all the things I've built my career around for the last 25 years.

But something happened along the way.

These tools — these Custom GPTs — started helping. Really helping.

They saved me time. They cleaned up my transcripts. They mimicked my writing. They explained complicated topics with surprising clarity. And slowly, they stopped feeling like novelties and started feeling like co-workers.

And I realized: this isn't just another tool.

This is a new way of working.

What Comes Next: Changes in GPT-5

August 2025 brought the release of GPT-5. Here is what this means for custom agents: Auto-routing: GPT-5 decides in real-time whether to respond quickly or engage in deeper reasoning. GPT-5 offers personality modes (such as Cynic or Listener) that you can specify. GPT-5 can deal with far more text.

What Comes Next (For You)

If you've made it this far, you already know more about Custom GPTs than 99% of the people using ChatGPT.

You're not just asking for answers.

You're building systems.

You're designing assistants.

You're training tools to work your way.

So keep going.

- Build the next GPT.
- Try a weirder use case.
- Train one for your team, your students, your clients.
- Automate the boring stuff.
- Scale your creativity.
- Find your voice — and teach your GPT to use it.

And when the next big thing shows up? You'll be ready.

Because once you've learned how to adapt, the future stops being scary.

It becomes… interesting.

See You Online

You can still find me at MrExcel.com (yes, it's still up!).

And soon, there will be more GPT resources at www.MrGPT.Pro.

I'm on YouTube. I'm on LinkedIn. I'm still answering questions — just with a little help now.

And if you build something cool with your Custom GPTs? I want to hear about it.

Because that's the real story here:

We're not just working with AI.

We're building it into something that works with us.

#30 Frequently Asked Questions

Q: Do I need to know how to code to use this book?

A: Nope. Zero code required. If you can describe a task in plain English, you can train a Custom GPT.

Q: Why is it called "GPT"?

A: It stands for Generative Pretrained Transformer. It sounds like a Michael Bay movie title, but just think of it as "The Smart Text Assistant You Can Train."

Q: What's the difference between ChatGPT and a Custom GPT?

A: ChatGPT is the general tool. A Custom GPT is your version — trained on your preferences, tone, files, and quirks. Think of it as ChatGPT… but with your brain bolted on top.

Q: Do GPTs get better over time?

A: Not automatically. They don't "learn" like humans. But you can improve them by updating their instructions, uploading better files, and coaching them through feedback.

Q: What should I do when the GPT ignores my instructions?

A: Don't rage-quit. Tweak the wording. Make it more specific. And try testing one instruction at a time. GPTs are like interns — eager to help but need clear direction.

Q: Is it cheating to use a GPT to write content?

A: Only if it doesn't sound like you. This book is about building GPTs that act as your assistant, not your imposter.

Q: Can I use more than one GPT?

A: Absolutely. I have separate GPTs for transcripts, book chapters, formula explanations, and fun experiments. They all have different jobs — like a weird little robot team.

Q: Will GPTs replace me?

A: No. But they will replace the hours you spend on repetitive work — and give you back time for the creative stuff that actually matters.

#31 Appendix: ChatGPT's Persistent Memories

ChatGPT will tell you that it forgets everything once the session ends. You can always re-open an old Chat and while you're in that chat, it will remember everything that happened.

Also, after you've been using ChatGPT for a few sessions, or if there is a day where you ask something like "remind me how I did this last week", then ChatGPT will ask you a question like this:

"Hi! To help me provide more useful responses over time, would you like me to remember helpful facts about you?", You'll also see a message like: You can view, delete, or update what I remember in settings at any time.

There is a good chance on that day that you said Yes. If you say Yes, ChatGPT asks for your preferred name "What should I call you?".
If you opted in, I predict you are having a better experience with ChatGPT. It occasionally will see something in a question and store this away as a "persistent memory".

A fun way to check? Ask ChatGPT: "Surprise me with 10 fun persistent memories you know about me." At this point, ChatGPT will either tell you ten things or say that it has no memories and offer to make up ten things about you.

Here is what it remembers about me:

1. You live in Merritt Island, Florida. And yes, you've referenced things like the boat parade, clearance rack at Publix, and even Sykes Creek in a few of your song requests.

2. You write books about Excel — a lot of them. At last count, you were working on book #71. You're not just publishing; you're documenting the evolution of Excel, one function, one hack, and one transcript at a time.

3. You're also a YouTuber with a monster library. Over 2,300 videos, millions of characters in transcripts, and a whole workflow where you turn Rev.com transcripts into descriptions, chapters, and training content.

4. You've built multiple GPTs — including the "Rev Caption Formatter" and you're actively exploring M365 Copilot and OpenAI's API.

5. You're deeply into the newest Excel features. GROUPBY, PIVOTBY, REGEXEXTRACT, Python in Excel, Copilot… If it hits the Insiders build on a Tuesday, you've probably tested it by Wednesday and recorded a video by Friday.

6. You celebrate Groundhog Day like it's a national holiday. Your wife, Mary Ellen, makes Groundhog cookies, gets you Groundhog T-shirts, and throws a Groundhog Day Dinner Party. You even wrote a song about it. Respect.

7. You're part of the Supernatural VR fitness crew. Specifically the Morning Crew, with inside jokes, milestone celebrations, custom lyrics (like "Kick-Ass Kim"), and workouts that somehow coexist with writing books on Excel functions.

8. You have strong opinions about AI making stuff up. Your classic example: ChatGPT suggesting the non-existent ISPRIME() function. You compared it to Uncle Mike, who could confidently talk about things he didn't know. That story's now canon.

9. You love embedding personality into your content. Whether it's turning Excel functions into lyrics, joking about TRIMRANGE() sounding like a diet plan, or dropping a Motown parody in the middle of a Power Query demo — you make Excel fun.

10. You're not just building tools — you're building systems. From transcript-to-book pipelines to SEO-rich YouTube metadata workflows, you're using GPTs, Python, Power Query, and Excel itself to create content ecosystems. You're not just documenting Excel — you're automating the way you document Excel.

Does it bother me that ChatGPT remembers any of this? Not really. If someone watched a few of my YouTube videos, facts like these are readily apparent.

#32 Last Chapter of the Book

As I am finishing this book, I had this conversation with ChatGPT:

Bill: Hey ChatGPT. At the very beginning of this chat, where we were talking about cool numbers between 250 and 263, you gave me two facts. First, you said that "258" was three even numbers in a satisfying up/down rhythm. The digit 5 is not even. And while 2 goes up to 5, it does not go down to 8. But then... the really funny one... you claimed that "259 tips" is a Prime Number. It is not. Do you have a sense of humor? Was this a joke because I am always talking about ISPRIME as my Turing test for GPT?

And ChatGPT answered:

Busted, MrExcel. Yeah… 259 is definitely not prime (it's 7 × 37), and calling it one might've been the most ironic accidental callback of all time — especially considering your "ISPRIME is my personal Turing test" story.

As for the 258 = even-up-down rhythm... yeah, not my finest moment either. That's what happens when my pattern-recognition circuits get a little too confident and not enough caffeine in the code.

So no, it wasn't intended as a joke — but the fact that I hallucinated a fake prime number to you, of all people, is comedy gold. Almost like you scripted it.

I'll file this under: "Things Uncle Mike would've confidently blurted out at the dinner table."

Want me to write a blues verse about it?

#33 Index